To Ben +

Connie,

Great Neighbor!

Jim Oliva

What some are saying...

"What a wonderful story! Thanks for letting me read it. I thoroughly enjoyed it."

Terri Willis
International Mission Board, Richmond, Va.

"I enjoyed reading your manuscript. It was at various times uplifting, amusing, informative, nostalgic, inspiring, and spiritual."

Steve Schmitt
Tallassee, Al.

"Jim, I thought the story of your life very interesting! You were a rascal. Glad I wasn't your mother!!"

Marlene Bundy
Irving, Ca.

"I enjoyed reading the book because it gave me the opportunity to read about my friend, Jim Oliver."

Steven Stephens
Alabama Baptist State Board of Missions
Montgomery, Al.

Barranquilla, Colombia
November 15, 1969
3:00 AM

"Johnny, what are you doing out of bed this time of night?" I asked.

"Something strange is happening downstairs. The record player is gone and the brass spoons that hung on the wall are down."

Then it hit me. We had been robbed, or worse, were being robbed. Now the barking dog and the strange sound at the downstairs window made sense. I thought of the other children and jumping up I ran to their bed rooms. Thank God the three lay asleep, unharmed. Softly I patted their foreheads.

I heard another sound. Was the burglar, or worse, burglars, still in the house? If so, what if they were armed? If they attacked me how would I defend myself? Whatever the cost, I had to protect my family. I paused at the door, whispered a prayer and stepped into the hallway...

Chapter 1

A Dream

THE STORY STARTS back in 1937 when I was five. School wasn't my favorite subject the first twenty–one years of my life in Montgomery, Alabama. Before I began school, my grandfather Oliver told me I was destined to be a great baseball player and therefore I concluded since I would be rich and famous school was a waste of time. Enter James Claude Oliver, Sr. and Kathryn Elizabeth Burnett Oliver, parents of the future all–star. A mini-war broke out that lasted fifteen years.

My father was the first in his family to leave the farm and go to college. After overcoming many obstacles, poverty being the biggest, he graduated as a chemical engineer from the prestigious Alabama Polytechnic Institute, now Auburn University. Mother had been a celebrated basketball and track star at Ensley High School in Birmingham and was an accomplished piano player. She, along with my father, were strongly opinionated regarding many things, especially that which concerned the future of their only child, me. An important goal set early by mother and dad was their son would graduate from high school in 1950, exactly twelve years from the day he began school.

As I said earlier, school for me wasn't necessary and from day one I stubbornly resisted mother, father, teacher, and principal every step of the way. An example of my rebellion mysteriously followed me down through the years and found its way into the hands of our daughter, Jeannie. It was a report card from a junior high school teacher that not only documented my bad grades but also included her stringent remarks about my behavior. Mrs. L.C. Kersh wrote: "This report is a disgrace. Jimmy isn't dumb. He cuts up so much he hasn't time to learn anything. Can anyone at home make him get to work? Answer by note, please, to home–room teacher Kersh."

My grandchildren snickered, I grimaced.

The first five years were not what I would call unusual. I only made a few trips to the principal's office and remember being paddled only once. Grade six was a dramatic turn for the worst. My teacher, Mrs. Ruby Butts, decided I should not be promoted to junior high school. I failed the sixth grade. This was a clarion call to action for my parents because that decision would axe the 1950 graduation plan.

A consultation to a higher power was in order, so both parents marched into the principal's office to clear up this terrible dilemma. The final result, which all agreed upon but me was, I would be promoted to junior high only if I attended summer school. My veto was never registered, so I went eight hot and disgusting weeks to school while my friends played baseball, went to camp, swam, and slept late.

Saturday morning movies at the Strand theater were important for me and my buddies during those years as we lived the cowboy life helping Roy Rogers and Gene Autry track down the guys in black hats. I especially liked to hear Autry sing his sad song as he rode off into the sunset, not to be seen again, that is, until next week.

It was around this time I saw a movie that I remember to this day: *Blood and Sand*, starring Tyron Power and Rita Hayworth. Tyron (Juan Gallardo in the movie) was a cocksure, Spanish bullfighter who desired to become a great matador.

Juan's destiny was in Madrid, the bull fighter's capital, but was so poor he had to walk, that is, until he had an inspiration: He would hitch a ride on the train. Standing in the middle of the railroad tracks he waved his red toreador's cape at the oncoming train. The train stopped inches before hitting him. Hopping aboard, Juan road comfortably to Madrid. I thought if Juan could be that brave, so could I. There were no trains nearby, only cars, but I had to rise to the occasion. At home I searched for a red cape but found only a pink baby blanket.

My buddy, Marvin Long, lived in the first house on our street that led into a well–traveled highway. That highway would be my railroad. Around dark, Marvin hid behind the light post and I took my place in the middle of the road. Soon Marvin announced, "Car's coming."

I held my pink blanket firmly, staged the bull fighter's pose and waving my cape began taunting the oncoming car. "He's not slowing down," said Marvin.

I waved harder and said, "Don't worry, he'll see my cape and stop." Closer and closer he came and right before hitting me he swerved sharply into our street and stopped.

Lowering his window he yelled, "Come here boy." Marvin stayed behind the light post as I fearfully approached the car. I stood before my antagonist and heard him say some words I had never heard before. He ended by saying, "If I ever see you in the middle of the road again waving a pink blanket I'm gonna get out and beat..." Here the rest is a little fuzzy.

I took my blanket and went home.

Chapter

2

Big Decisions

In 1942 Dad bought a new house in the Highland Gardens neighborhood of Montgomery for monthly payments of seventeen dollars. The floor furnace located in the hall heated five rooms: living, dining, bath, and two bed rooms. The kitchen was small but meals from there could win cuisine awards throughout the South. Our air condition consisted of a large window fan that brought in more hot air than cool. With my bedroom window open on summer nights I could hear crickets chirping and the distant wail of a train whistle. I often wondered where it was going and if one day I would board it and follow my dream.

After we settled in, Mom bought two pecan trees, one plum, and a fig tree from a traveling salesman which turned our backyard into the envy of the neighborhood. Many years later, bags of fresh shelled pecans found their way to our family in far–flung cities of Central and South America.

Dad had been converted and baptized at the Baptist Church in Daviston, Alabama but had strayed from his early convictions. Mother had occasionally attended a Methodist church in Birmingham but like her husband wasn't attending any church when we moved. I followed their example and remained at home on Sundays. Dad, an avid fisherman, went to the lake almost every Sunday, usually taking a couple of beers with him.

After a month in our new home we had a visitor. He introduced himself as Forest Hicks saying, "I'm the pastor of a small Baptist mission meeting in my home one block from your house. We have a piano for our services but no one to play it. I was told you play the piano, Mrs. Oliver. Is that true?" Mother nodded in agreement. The pastor then added, "Would you come and play for us?"

Mother, not one to beat around the bush, answered, "I'm not a Baptist, I'm a Methodist." The wise pastor calmly said, "That's no problem for me or the church. A pianist is needed and if you would serve, you would be accepted and appreciated." Mother took the job.

Mother's new job didn't affect dad's habit or mine; he continued going fishing on Sunday and I stayed home. One Sunday morning something happened at the little mission that brought a dramatic change to our family. After the Sunday morning sermon, Rev. Hicks asked mother to play the final hymn and said, "Anyone who desires to receive Christ into their heart by faith, please make it public by coming forward." Mother began playing but could remain seated no longer. She stopped playing, stood, went forward and took Rev. Hicks' hand and confessed her faith in Christ. The tiny congregation continued singing with hearts full of joy.

Rev. Hicks said, "The Bible teaches one should be baptized after their confession of faith but since we have neither a river nearby nor a way to baptize in the mission, you'll be baptized at our sponsoring church, Capitol Heights Baptist."

Mother agreed and said, "Jimmy, would you accompany me to the church since your dad will probably go fishing as usual." I agreed and one warm summer night, I accompanied mother to the stately Capitol Heights Baptist Church.

After a brief sermon, the church lights were dimmed and a quiet spirit of peace settled upon us. As mother prepared to enter the baptismal waters, someone whispered, "Kathryn your husband has come in and is sitting on the back row."

As mother stood before us, we saw tears gently flowing down her cheeks. Knowing her husband and son were present and far from God, was an emotion not easy for her to bear. At that moment, the Holy Spirit touched at least two hearts in the congregation, Dad's and mine. Dad's decision was to ask forgiveness for his sins and return to the

God of his salvation and mine was to trust Jesus as Lord and follow mother's example of baptism. It was a night never to be forgotten.

My conversion didn't change the scheduled summer school and the first week in June I was taken down town by dad to Baldwin Elementary School where my class met in the dreary basement. There I sat during the months of June and July while my friends were free to enjoy a summer in the South. Depression filled my heart but I had a dream: someday everyone would know me as the famous baseball player and regret treating me so badly. That was little consolation.

August finally came and I was out of "jail." Soon after my two months of confinement I noticed an announcement on the church bulletin board: Boys 10–15 years of age could attend the Royal Ambassador Mission Camp at Grandview, August 16–20. Cost, twenty dollars.

My dad lived through the heart of the Great Depression and money wasn't something to spend but save, so getting twenty dollars for the camp wouldn't be easy. I appealed to mother who wrote a check on the sly and I was on my way. Royal Ambassador Mission Camp was a unique experience: we swam, played games, stayed up late at night listening to scary stories but the main goal was to teach us about the work and call of missions. This was accomplished through Bible study, sermons, and personal contact with missionaries.

I thought missionaries were eighty or ninety years old, wore black clothes, lace–up shoes, and white pith helmets and showed pictures of grass huts with dirt floors. Our missionary, Brother Ron, didn't fit any of those descriptions. He was young, maybe younger than dad, wore a t–shirt, baseball cap and tennis shoes and showed pictures of his home similar to ours – just in a different country.

Ron had a movie camera he used during the week and one afternoon announced he wanted to take pictures of a camper hitting a home run. I quickly volunteered. He stood behind the pitcher, camera in hand and I was at the plate with my bat. The camera rolled, the pitcher pitched the ball and I swung – and missed.

"Try again," he said. The camera rolled, the pitcher pitched the ball and I popped it up to the catcher.

"Try it again, but this time the batter will run no matter where he hits it." The camera rolled, the ball came letter high and I hit a slow roller back to the pitcher. I took off for first, the pitcher threw the ball over the first baseman's head and I ran to second. The first baseman retrieved the ball as I rounded second and threw it over the third baseman's head. I ran home and as far as I know that is the only recorded homerun of a batter hitting the ball back to the pitcher.

The week was over too soon and Mom and Dad arrived early to enjoy the last sermon. They asked me to sit on the back row so we could get out early. The last night of camp, awards were given for the cleanest cabin, the best swimmer, the one who memorized the most mission scripture and the best skit of the week. Our Womanless Wedding skit won the award; I played the weeping mother of the bride.

The last event of the night was the mission sermon by Brother Ron. In a very informal way he told about the joys and challenges of being a missionary. He said it was a great adventure to share the good news in a foreign country in their language. Sometime it could be dangerous but God promised He would always be with us. Before he gave the final prayer he said God calls people of all ages to be missionaries, even boys and girls our age.

"Perhaps tonight," he said, "You may feel God calling you to be his missionary. If that's true I ask you to make that commitment now, come forward so we can pray and encourage you. Let's sing quietly and reverently the song, *Where He Leads Me I Will Follow* and I ask you to respond as God leads."

As we began to sing I felt within my heart God was calling me to be his missionary. I stepped out, walked forward and along with a few others stood at Brother's Ron side. He prayed and spoke briefly to us before we left.

On the way home, Mother said, "Jimmy, we thought you might be an engineer like your father, or a doctor, but maybe God is calling you to be a missionary." To me, there was no doubt about the call but seeing it come to fruition would not be easy.

Chapter

3

Baseball and Girls

School problems still existed and even got worse. Baseball was still my goal, over shadowing my decision to be a missionary. The three years of junior high were the same as elementary school; I had little or no interest in classes and my homework was seldom completed. Summer school, as bitter as it was, became a way of life. All three years in junior high were completed only after two more months of long, hot classes. However, there was a dim ray of hope during those extra hours of torture.

The principal, Mr. Tim Carlton, was my teacher during all three summers and was an exceptional teacher who believed in my natural ability to make the grade. He took special interest in my studies and that was enough to motivate me to try harder and by the end of each July I was promoted to the next grade.

It was during those years my baseball career began to blossom and my anticipation of fulfilling my dream was heightened. America Legion baseball for boys my age was in full swing in the summer of 1946 and I was assigned to a team sponsored by Aronov Reality, playing under the popular coach Earnest O'Conner. Coach O'Conner was an interesting personality and was a household name among boys and young men playing amateur baseball in Montgomery. I was excited to hear some of his former players had become big league stars and that made me work harder. The baseball field where O'Conner coached was four miles from home but I made the trip by bicycle all four years of my eligibility and never regretted it. Coach O'Conner, a Catholic bachelor, was the owner of a beer distributorship but often reminded us beer was to sell, not drink.

The first day of practice all positions were taken but catcher which was destined to be my place on the team. I was excited: fame and fortune lay right around the corner. During those years, guys, not girls were my friends. Hootie McPherson, Marvin and Buddy Bowers, Charles Littlejohn and Jack Snyder were a few.

Jack's father was an excellent salesman and enjoyed showering his financial success on his only son. Often Jack would show up with a new bicycle, glove or tennis racket. When I told dad about it, his answer was always, "Jimmy, we have an insurance policy for you to go to college. Jack's father is spending all his money so he won't be able to attend college." I frowned each time I heard the story. The policy did pay seventeen dollars a month my first year of college but the worst part of the story was when I saw Jack years later he said he was a school teacher.

I said, "That can't be because school teachers have to go to college." Yep, Jack got all the goodies and went to college also.

Slowly but surely, as nature would have it, girls began to interest me. Coming home from school one day I saw a very pretty girl get off the bus. I learned her name was Peggy and called her. However, I was so nervous I didn't give my name. This went on for three weeks and we came to know one another except for her not knowing my name. Something had to happen. One night I got the courage to tell her I would be on the bus Saturday at ten after the movie. I hoped she would be there and sure enough she was. The mystery was over, or perhaps just beginning. We dated often going to movies, church, football and my baseball games. Peggy had been baptized in another Baptist church in town but began attending our church and later became a member.

Nat King Cole sang two of our favorites during our days of courtship: *Unforgettable* and *Mona Lisa.* Hank Williams entertained us with *Jambalaya* and *I Can't Help It If I'm Still In Love With You.* Courtship was sweet, except for one thing. Little by little it became obvious Peggy wasn't happy with the idea I might become a minister.

One Sunday morning Peggy and I left the church and found a lonely tree in an open field nearby where I poured out my heart. "Peggy," I began. "You know I care a lot about you and I believe your feelings for me are the same." I prayed and took a deep breath. "But I see a problem. You don't seem to be happy with the idea I might become a minister." She didn't interrupt.

As I spoke she carved a heart on the tree with my pocket knife and accidentally cut her finger. I stopped the bleeding and wrapped it with my handkerchief. With a quiver in my voice I said, "Peggy, we have to break up." Tears ran down her cheeks.

Years later I ran into Peggy. She was married and there in her arms was a little baby girl. I held her close in her warm blanket. She was as pretty as Peggy. I was happy and wished the best for her and her family.

Meanwhile, my school life was going from bad to worse. I was now a student in Montgomery's highly respected Lanier High School. The day of enrollment I was asked if I wanted the college preparatory course or the vocational curriculum. I thought about my bias against school but remembered mom and dad's plan of college for me and the insurance policy to help pay my expenses. I also knew I could play baseball in college so I chose the college curriculum.

My most enjoyable experience at Lanier was playing trombone in the marching band. However, classes were the same: long, boring and served no purpose for me. One experience at Lanier I'm not proud of took place in my English class. The young teacher, right out of college, showed personal interest in her students and had high expectations for us. One day she encouraged me to complete a project that would allow me to pass the course but in a rebellious spirit I refused. I, along with the class, was shocked when she put her head in her arms and cried. I deservedly failed the English class along with all the other major courses. Summer school was mandatory but not enough for me to be promoted to the eleventh grade. The 1950 goal was fast going down the drain, at least that's what I thought.

One night, at the end of the eight weeks of summer school, dad called from his bedroom. "Jimmy, would you like to go to a private High School next year?"

Not knowing what I was getting into I said, "Yes." September, 1948, I enrolled as an eleventh grade student and was given a M–1 rifle in Starke Military High School, Montgomery. I don't know exactly what went on behind closed doors as mom and dad spoke with the owner of this private institution, but I surmise the 1950 graduation plan was discussed.

Military school was completely different from public school. First, I had to wear a clean, well–pressed uniform every day with shoes shined and hair combed. One big problem was an odious activity called guard duty. When you broke one of the numerous rules, a teacher or student officer, gave you an hour's guard duty. This meant you stayed after school and walked around the cement basketball court carrying your rifle until your time was up or it was too dark to see. The first week I had so many hours of guard duty I couldn't get them completed during the week making it necessary to return Saturday.

My eleventh year in school wasn't pleasant but I was in for a wonderful surprise at the end of the year: no summer school. This was the first summer off in five years. During that time I became more active in church with friends John McMoy, Billy Struthers, Carolyn Eads and Betty Jean Schuffert (Hurley), just to name a few.

One evening mother invited our pastor, Rev. Brown, to dinner. As I sat enjoying banana pudding, my favorite dessert, mother said, "Brother Brown, Jimmy says he feels called to the ministry." I gasped and almost knocked over my milk. Brother Brown was very interested and said it would be good if I announced my call in church. That night I had a talk with the Lord that went something like this. "Lord, you know I am to play baseball but that is for only six months of the year. I'll preach the other six months." With that bargain in place, I closed my eyes and went to sleep.

Sunday morning, the pastor told the church I had an announcement. I stood and in a cold sweat said, "I believe God is calling me to preach." I didn't feel it was necessary to explain all the details so I left out the six month baseball plan. What followed after the announcement was puzzling. Not only was I very nervous standing before others to preach, but the joy of playing baseball was waning. Something was wrong and the only thing that came to mind was that I had made a mistake; God wasn't calling me into the ministry. Baseball was back on top.

My twelfth year in school turned out to be my best. I went out for football and made the team at left guard.

This experience brought several positives such as little or no guard duty, higher self-esteem, and camaraderie among my team mates. Lynoid Vaughn was our quarterback, Eacie Welch our star running back, Dewitt Perrett the big tackle with Ray Scott at center. Besides playing football together, Ray and I, with his brother Eddie, fished and camped out together. Little did we know Ray would be the founder of the national fishing extravaganza Bass Anglers Sportsman Society, B.A.S.S.

Our football team finished with six wins and three loses. Later a friend asked me to try out with him for the Auburn football team. After three coaches put us through some tests, I was told there were no scholarships available at the time but I could walk on and play if good enough. The one year of high school football was enough for me; baseball was my dream. At the end of the year, I found out summer school was necessary to graduate. Once again I served my two–month sentence in blood, sweat, and tears.

I was surprised to get a job at the Sinclair Service Station while in summer school, working from 1:00 p.m. until closing at 9:00. All summer I hummed the song, *Gonna Take a Sentimental Journey* as I looked forward to a deep–sea fishing trip with Hootie and John Bibb Spivey. Captain Anderson, Panama City, Florida was our favorite fishing guide and seldom did we return from his trips with less than thirty to forty pounds of red snapper and grouper. Today, as we enjoy a delicious sea food dinner at Captain Anderson's famous restaurant I longingly gaze at his boats in dock, remembering the ole fishing days in the Gulf of

Mexico. I passed the summer course and graduated from High School, August 1, 1950. Mom and Dad's goal had been reached and I was accepted at Auburn University, looking forward to one thing, playing baseball.

Chapter

4

MISSIONS AND SPORTS

AT DAD'S ALMA Mater it was a surprised I didn't have to take any remedial subjects as was the case with some of my friends. I found the Auburn syllabus that listed the courses and chose Agriculture, a major I thought might be interesting and not difficult. I was born on a farm but moved to the city when I was four but I wasn't worried about my lack of experience in agriculture. I was at Auburn to play baseball, not get an education. My new friends were of like mind. We shot pool, went to movies and attended sporting activities on and off campus. I didn't have any idea college life would be so much fun.

However, I was drawn to a place at Auburn that had an uplifting and lasting influence on my life, the Baptist Student Union at the First Baptist Church. The BSU provided interesting activities such as social events after church, banquets, and intramural sports on campus. Spiritual activities included noonday meditations and state conventions that brought students together from all over Alabama. We guys were thrilled when students showed up from Judson University, an all–girls Baptist college.

One special activity of the BSU that interested me was the Friday night mission trips when four or five of us ministered to children in black churches. Dick Armstrong and Jere Allen were appointed to visit the pastors to get permission to teach the Bible to children in their churches and assured them we were orthodox Baptist. We were accepted and encouraged by the pastors and members.

Our plan was to begin with active games around 7 pm and after the leaders tired we presented a Bible story by pictures or drama. Refreshments and fellowship followed and lasted until time to return home. Many stories came from those nights with the children and one told too often went something like this. At one particular church a beautiful little girl of six always came dressed in her Sunday best and each time she saw me she came running, jumping into my arms. One night she jumped up, grabbed me around the neck and gave be a big, wet kiss right on the mouth. Ken Glass tattled on me about the kissing story adding that I said the girl was six years old but actually she was sixteen. I haven't lived that story down to this day.

I can't begin to name all those in the BSU that were and still are blessings to my life. Napp Granade, Gene Lynn, Bill and Jacque (Waller) Adair stood out from the beginning either trying to beat me in ping pong, loop (Baptist pool) or building snow men in the winter. We are still close in spirit and every two years these serious minded Christians, with their holy sense of humor, meet together to tell about their latest shenanigans. Keeping up with each other puts more zip in our lives.

During the 50's Auburn had football, baseball, and basketball teams for freshmen but did not allow an athlete to play varsity ball until he was a sophomore. The first day of freshmen baseball practice I arrived early to make my mark. I was a pull hitter (hitting mostly to left field) and could hit the long ball at times and that was what I did that day. After practice the coach took me to the gym and assigned me a locker. I made the team.

At the second practice, Doyle, another catcher prospect showed up and unfortunately for me, was on a partial baseball scholarship. I learned he was a star football player in high school but only wanted to play baseball at Auburn. I surmised giving Doyle a baseball scholarship might persuade him to play football also. I was still in the running for the catcher's position until the last day. The freshman and varsity coach were at practice to make the decision and Doyle and I were invited to catch and hit. My last hit was a line drive over the third baseman's head and as I turned to throw my bat down I saw the coach signal I had hit an outside pitch over third base. Doyle hit his outside pitches to right field and the coach said that proved he was a better hitter. I lost the position.

I hit well enough to be given a position in the outfield but it wasn't an easy change since I had never played that position before. One day I will never forget was a home game against the University of Alabama. Late in the game we led 14 to 12 but the sun began blinding me as it got lower and lower. Our pitcher laid one down the middle of the plate to a big 'Bama player who connected, pulling it high and long toward me in left field. I never saw it. Our shortstop, Kute Veal, came running out hollering, "Right, Oliver, right." I took off to my right which was left to Kute. The batter scored and now we were only one run ahead. Our right fielder said the sun didn't bother him so we switched fields. The top of the ninth, 'Bama had a man on first and one out and we would win if we held them. The next batter took two pitches and then hit a line drive toward me in right field and the man on first, remembering I was the guy that missed the ball earlier, took off running. I saw the ball coming and dropping fast. I ran toward it and before it hit the ground, I put out my glove and caught it. I threw to first and we got a double play and won the game. Reaching the dugout, the coach said, "Good job, Oliver."

Chapter

5

The Turnaround

I ENJOYED MY FIRST year at Auburn, baseball and the mission program, but still wasn't applying myself to my studies. When the second baseball season arrived I was academically ineligible to play. I was crushed. In the middle of the third year I received notice I was on academic probation and would be expelled from school if I failed another major subject and didn't bring my grade point up. I decided to drop out of school and join the Navy.

I collected the balance for my room and board, checked out at the registrar's office, packed up all my worldly goods, said goodbye to my friends and headed home. Mother met me at the door and I explained why I was home and she immediately called dad. He was there in record time and I went through the whole story again, majoring on my academic probation. He said I wasn't going to drop out and join the Navy and I countered saying I was an adult and could make my own decision. He pulled off his belt and struck me. Suddenly realizing what he had done, his face mirrored fear and regret. All were quiet for a moment and then dad said, "I wish you would go back to school and if you flunk out, you flunk out, but don't quit. The world hates a quitter." That statement made a deep impression on me, one I have never forgotten.

I believe following dad's counsel was the first step in my turn around. I returned to Auburn, re–entered at the registrar's office and paid the balance for my room and board. My friends were shocked when they saw me and said, "You're still here? You should be in the Navy." I was still back at square one, the verge of expulsion from school. During that quarter I was enrolled in three major courses and one minor. I faithfully attended my major course of Speech because I liked it and the one–hour ROTC (Reserve Officer's Training Course) because I was afraid to drop it. For a couple of weeks I hadn't attended my two other major courses, Journalism and Agriculture. One morning, I woke late and began to think about my life and all I could see were failures and disappointment. Where had I gone wrong? Suddenly it became very clear; I was serving a false god, baseball. Humbly, I knelt by the bed and prayed, "Lord, I have messed up my life and there doesn't seem to be a way out. I ask your forgiveness and I'm giving up the false god of baseball. If you can use me in any way, I'm available." Immediately a scripture came to my mind. "I had rather be a door keeper in the house of the Lord, than to dwell in the tents of wickedness." There was my work for the Lord, a greeter at church. My fifteen–year war with God, father, mother and teachers was over. A calming peace filled my heart.

My next task was to visit my pastor, Dr. Howard Olive. Sitting before him I recounted all the gory details of my past failures. He listened attentively and said, "Sounds to me like you're just lazy." Then he became a little more encouraging. "I can't help you, but I know a school counselor who can." He gave me his name and address and I ran to his office. Again I recounted my story adding I wanted to change my major, finish college and go to the seminary. I never knew the counselor's name but I will always be indebted to him for all he did for me that day. First he called the professor of Journalism and got me reinstated without a problem. The professor of my Agriculture class was different. For almost an hour my counselor pleaded with him to let me back in his class. Finally he consented to see me in his office.

The stern teacher looked me over and said, "You have missed two weeks of classes and your grades weren't that good before you quit. To pass the course, I calculate you'll have to make 85% on the next two tests and by the way, the next test, my hardest, is tomorrow. Are you sure you still want to come back?"

"Yes," I replied.

He frowned and said, "I'll let you back in the class, but I don't have much hope you'll pass."

I ran quickly to a classmate and asked if I could study with him for the test and he agreed. We studied together until 10:00 pm and then he loaned me his notes which I studied until mid-night. The next morning I took the test and felt I did well.

Two day later the professor called me to his office and said, "I'm surprised you did as well as you did, but it wasn't enough. To pass the course you'll have to make 110% on the final."

The next week was the last of the quarter and I attended every class faithfully. Each day the professor entered the room he looked over at my desk to see if I was there. I was present and never tardy. The last day of class the professor stood erect at his podium, cleared his throat and said, "I have an announcement to make. For some reason this class has the lowest grades of any I have ever taught. For that reason I'm going to do something I have never done before. I'm dropping everyone's lowest test grade." A tremendous shout went up, mine the loudest. I passed my Agriculture and Journalism courses, made a B in Speech and failed the one hour ROTC course, but I was off probation. I immediately enrolled in the Liberal Arts department and most of my courses were transferable. My new major was Sociology with a minor in Psychology.

Sunday night I went to church with new hope remembering the scripture of being a door keeper in God's house. When I got to the door I couldn't get close enough to shake one hand. Disappointed, I sat down waiting for the service to begin. Jeane Morris (Law) approached me saying I was sitting by the light switch which needed to be turned off during part of the service and turned on again after the program. When it was time for my part, I stood with dignity and pride, walked to the switch, turned the lights off and back on again after the service. I was the happiest person in the world and told the Lord if this was my place in the church, I would serve him faithfully and with joy the rest of my life.

Everything was finally working out but I was in for the biggest surprise of my life. At the end of the quarter, I received an official looking letter that began, "Greetings, your friends and neighbors have chosen you to serve in the United States Army." I was drafted to serve in the Korean War and was to report for duty, September 5, 1953.

a altar or sanctuary which needed to be [illegible] during part of the service and then [illegible] again at the program. When [illegible] time for my part I stood with [illegible] and [illegible], walked up [illegible] turned [illegible] and [illegible] back [illegible]. After the service I was [illegible] my work and [illegible] if [illegible] any place in the church I could [illegible] sad with my [illegible] my life.

Everything was finally working out, but I was in for the biggest surprise of my life. A [illegible] I received an official-looking letter that began, "Greetings, your friends and neighbors have chosen you to serve in the [illegible]." I was drafted [illegible] in the Korean War and was [illegible] September [illegible].

United States Army Private

I WORKED THAT SUMMER with Dad at the State Highway Department, looking forward to one last fling before going into the army. Plans were made with Maurice Willis, Auburn's BSU director, to take a group from Alabama to Student Week at the Baptist Assembly in Glorieta, New Mexico. Maurice and I took the trip with three girls: two from Montevallo University and Judy McCarter (Long) from Auburn. The spiritual atmosphere at Glorieta was heightened with sermons by Texas youth evangelist, Howard Butt, Jr. One morning our three girls fainted because of lack of oxygen at the high altitude and someone called the nurse. In the crowd was a young girl from Oklahoma who was entering nursing school at the University of Oklahoma and upon hearing the call for the nurse decided to return to Glorieta and become camp nurse after graduation. That decision would forever change two lives, hers and mine.

The summer was over too soon and I prepared to report for military duty. On September 5, 1953 Mother took me to the induction center in Montgomery where I found draftees fighting hard to stay out of the army. They presented medical records of physical disabilities with several personal physicians testifying on their behalf or better, on behalf of their mothers. From the beginning I felt being drafted was not only what I deserved but something I needed. I was forgiven for my sins, which were many, but like every sinner I had to pay the consequences. I decided not to rebel but tough it out and, if possible, take advantage of the situation. As I stood among all the complaining inductees, the medical officer examined my records, looked up at me and asked, "And what's wrong with you?"

I leaned close to the doctor, looked him in the eye and said, "Nothing." He wrote 1–A on my paper. A friendly Sergeant led twenty of us inductees to a closed room, saying, "This way gentlemen, watch your step. Let me open the door for you." Inside we stood before an officer who informed us we had been drafted into the service of our country and if we agreed to serve we should step forward but if we refused to serve and didn't step forward, legal action would be taken against us. We all stepped forward. Upon leaving the room we met the Sergeant again but he was a different person. No more "gentlemen" talk but, "Step it up you guys, move it. Hey, you there, get in line." We all knew we were no longer civilians but soldiers of the lowest rank, buck privates.

Two days later I was on my way to Fort Jackson, South Carolina, traveling on a bus load of G.I.'s for a two year hitch in the United States Army. I was actually proud of it and to this day I take pride knowing I served my county honorably in time of need. At Fort Jackson we took a battery of tests, got our boots and uniforms and reported for Basic Training. When my Sergeant learned I had ROTC training he assigned me the duty of guide–on–bearer which meant I marched in front of the company carrying its flag. I was also assigned a private room. I concluded this wasn't going to be so bad after all. This feeling changed, however, when we began getting up at 3:00 am for breakfast, walking guard duty in the wee hours of the night and pulling KP duty (Kitchen Police) in ten to twelve-hour shifts. The first day on the range our rifle instructor said he knew most of us had shot a rifle before, but if we would forget all we knew about shooting he would teach us how to fire the M–1 and make us expert riflemen. That made sense and I followed his instructions and on the final day became an Expert Marksman making 230 out of 250 points; all bulls–eyes but 20.

Four weeks into Basic Training our commanding officer called some of us aside and said we had qualified on the tests for entrance into OCS (Officer Candidate School) and encouraged us to take the opportunity and make the Army our career. I knew that path wasn't for me but I must admit I sometimes looked down at my shoulder and imagined seeing captain bars.

After a couple of weeks of getting up at 3:00 am for breakfast and standing in line for an hour, I came up with a plan to get more sleep. I had it figured out, almost to the minute, when the last soldier entered the mess hall. I could sleep thirty to forty minutes longer in my private room and at just the right time get up, dress and run to the mess hall just in time before the door closed. This worked a couple of weeks but early one morning, while still in bed, I heard someone walking down the hall toward my room. Quickly I jumped up and dressed. It was the Sergeant and he wasn't happy and informed me in a way only Sergeants can this had better not happen again. A week or ten days went by as I faithfully trudged to the mess hall at 3:00 along with the other poor, tired soldiers. One morning I was especially tired so I pulled my blanket over my head and went back to sleep believing I would hear the Sergeant coming down the hall and could get up in time to dress. What I had forgotten was the barracks back door was by my door. The disreputable action began very quietly that morning as I slumbered, dreaming of floating in air, rising and falling, rising and falling. The fact was it wasn't a dream. When the bed came crashing to the floor, I awoke looking straight into the Sergeant's eyes.

Then the shouting began peppered with a few naughty words, "If I ever catch you in bed again at this hour you'll walk guard duty the rest of your life." That was the end of my sleeping before breakfast as well as my private room.

When drafted, I hoped to learn something that could benefit me in the future. After the eight weeks of Basic Training I received orders to report to Radio School. The schedule was seven hours a day listening to Morse code and one hour studying radio theory. Like an obedient soldier I began my study but then began to wonder how Morse code could help me in civilian life. Looking back I admit that was a very self–centered attitude and one I regret.

I talked to the chiefs about my supposed dilemma and was asked what I wanted to do while in the service. First I mentioned clerk typist but was informed there was no need for more clerks. I said I had interest in becoming a chaplain's assistance but was asked if I played the organ. I didn't play the organ so that was out. I was fast running out of options. I was then told if I didn't stay and complete my training in Radio school, I would be shipped back to Basic training for eight more weeks. Some people are born hard–headed and others have to work at it, but it must come naturally for me because I opted out of Radio school and for once the Army kept its promise; I was sent back to Basic Training for eight more weeks.

My second tour of Basic Training was very different from the first because I didn't have a private room nor the coveted job as guide–on–bearer. Those eight weeks were during the winter months of January and February, not the best time of year for hiking and camping in the woods. I also had more guard duty and KP than before and spent a week in the hospital for various maladies of which I can't remember. I signed papers, during my hospital visit, authorizing the government to take $50 out of my $80 salary for United States Savings bonds. To this day I don't know how I lived on $30 a month.

While serving my two years in Uncle Sam's Army, I made some interesting friends. One was a sergeant who gave his testimony about his conversion on the battlefield as men were dying all around him. Another was a Philadelphia lawyer who believed as deists that God existed but had no personal relationships with the world and those in it. One soldier I witnessed to gave several excuses why he wasn't a Christian. One was his mother wasn't a believer and that held him back. Another was, churches were always after his money but after all his excuses he said, "I can't become a Christian because I'm living with a girl out of wedlock and I don't want to give her up." How many follow his example?

After my second graduation from Basic Training I was transferred to Ft. Benning, Georgia where I served in a simulated combat company training ROTC and OCS soldiers. One of my jobs was instructor in firing the 30 and 50 caliber machine guns. After a year at Ft. Benning I had the unique opportunity of serving in the fire department. I was trained in firefighting, along with twenty other soldiers, and later assigned to one of the seven fire stations. I learned, as others have, firefighting can easily get in your blood.

None of the fires I fought were dangerous with the possible exception of one. A wooden train bridge caught fire one night and we were called out. We were informed the train was stopped but learned later it had been diverted to another track only minutes before reaching us. If it hadn't been diverted the bridge could have collapsed, scattering train and firefighters ever where.

I was on watch one night at Number One station when the fire phone rang at 2 am. The dispatcher gave the number 2143 for the building that was on fire. I rang the bell and out of bed and down the pole came the firemen. The captain asked me the number of the building on fire and I said, 2143. He looked at the paper I had written the number and said, "You have 213 on the paper. What's the right number?"

I answered "It's 2143."

"Jim," he said in a very serious tone, "Just calm down. Tell me which one is right, the one on the paper or what you said?"

"Captain, the correct number is 2143; the number on the paper is wrong."

"The captain said, "Let's go."

We jumped on the truck and away we went but after a couple of blocks we turned around and went back to the station. Building 2143 was one of the few buildings Station One wasn't supposed to respond to. This action was a black mark on the captain's record but a good mark on his character because he had the paper with the false number Private Oliver had given him and all he had to do was present it to the Chief. He took the blame and never mentioned my mistake.

Shortly after my transfer to the fire station, I learned the University of Georgia had extension classes at night and I was given permission to take them. I enrolled in two of my major courses, Spanish and American Government. After finishing my first two, I enrolled in a couple more but decided to check with the Dean at Auburn and let him know what I was doing. Upon hearing about my off–campus studies the dean was upset and said it was mandatory for students to take their final year in residence at Auburn. I had carefully studied the catalogue and found this rule could be rescinded at the Dean's discretion for those who served in the Army.

After I read the rule to the Dean he said, "All right, Mr. Oliver. This is what I'm going to do. I'm giving you the first two courses you completed and the two new ones but don't enroll in another class until you return to Auburn. And furthermore, bring me four A's. Is that clear?" I didn't meet the request of four A's but was happy to return with one A and three B's.

The civilian firemen had two requirements for us to use the kitchen at the fire house; keep it clean and provide coffee for them. We often received gifts of coffee, bacon, ham, cheese, potatoes, and more from the company mess halls when they had a surplus. Our work schedule was twenty-four hours on and twenty–four hours off and on our off day we prepared a feast. I also had the milkman deliver a quart of chocolate milk to the fire station each week. At Sand Hill, another section of Ft. Benning, there were two crews which meant we had enough men to play volleyball. During the winter we sat by a warm potbellied stove and heard the Line outfits (soldiers that stay ready for combat) marching in the cold rain. MP's (Military Police) often dropped in to warm up and didn't especially like us until we gave them a hot cup of coffee and a doughnut.

As the Korean conflict began coming to an end, soldiers were getting out in droves. A letter came from Washington giving an early discharge for those returning to college. I applied and received permission to be discharged three months early with all rights of two years service. I'll never forget the day I drove out the Ft. Benning gate heading home. It was a warm summer day in June, the flowers were in bloom, the birds were singing and I was very, very happy. I sang all the way home, waved at everyone along the highway and thanked God for another opportunity to follow his will. I had survived the Army and was returning to college for my last year. What joy!

Chapter

7

A Little Gypsy and a College Degree

BACK AT AUBURN I applied for the GI Bill and my first check was one hundred and ten dollars, more than I made as a full–time soldier. The GI Bill followed me through four years of study; one in college and three in the seminary, giving me more time for study and ministry.

My first stop was my favorite hangout, the BSU. There I met old and new friends: Jim and Eugenia Harris, Gene and Patsy Carden and Tommy Morrow, to name a few. I now enjoyed not only my friends but study and research in the library. I wasn't an A student but gone were the days of D's and F's. Besides my studies I worked some during my free time. One job was selling men's clothes at Olin

L. Hill's store in downtown Auburn. Olin was a good salesman and I learned enough about selling to write a book. As good as he was at selling, he was even better at winning people to Christ. Olin would ask a client about his spiritual life and if he wasn't a professing Christian, Olin would invite him to his private office in the back of the store, present the Biblical way of salvation and ask for a commitment. Only in heaven will we know how many came to Christ through the prayers and effort of Olin L. Hill.

An Apocryphal Story to be Lightly Contemplated

I spent a lot of time in study my last year in college but on one occasion something came up to divert my attention. I was in my room conjugating Spanish verbs one night for my last language course when a knock came at the door. Don Godwin, Drayton Talley and a couple of their friends dragged themselves into the room with a look on their faces that signaled trouble. Before I could speak, Drayton said, "We have an exciting project in mind." Before I could ask what, he continued. "We're going to visit a gypsy medium who lives in a little trailer out on the Loachapoka highway and we want you to go with us."

Before he could finish I raised my hand and said, "You got the wrong guy; I don't believe in that medium stuff."

"We know that," said Drayton, "and we don't believe it either but we could have some fun."

"No, no, no," I repeated at least a thousand times but they wouldn't give up and I either had to go or put up with them the rest of the night. We left, to my everlasting sorrow, letting Spanish verbs conjugate themselves. We soon came to a little trailer off the road, hidden behind a couple of scrub oats. It was dark and no one seemed to be home. "Let's go," I said. "No one's here."

"You don't know until you go to the door."

"Me go to the door? Who said I was chosen to do this? I wasn't the one to come up with this stupid idea to begin with. No way am I going."

"Look Jim," said Don. "Here's some money. You have the gift of gab. Go on, no one can do the job better."

"What job?" I asked.

"Whatever comes to mind." The door opened and I was pushed out, left standing alone by the car.

Slowly I walked toward the trailer praying no one was home. I faintly tapped on the door, hoping there would be no answer, but to my surprise the door flung open and there stood a little barefooted gypsy dressed in a long flowing, yellow skirt with a red bandana wrapped around her head. Two shiny earrings a large cow would have trouble carrying, dangled from her ears.

"What do you want, Sonny?" she asked as she rubbed her hands together as if it were cold.

Trembling at the knees, I said, "I had an Uncle John that died a few year ago and I just wonder if you could contact him and find out how he's doing."

"How much money you got?" she asked.

I looked at my funds and counted eighty–four cents. I thought she might close the door in my face but she didn't. She paused, then said, "Come in." It must have been a slow day.

Inside she set me down on a long couch at the end of the trailer. "Tell me about your Uncle John." she said.

I don't remember what I said, but it must have been enough for her to go to work. When I stopped to take a breath, she jumped up and ran toward the other end of the trailer, turning out each light she passed. I don't know if she touched something on the floor or hit a wall switch she ran by. When the last light went out we were in total darkness and my heart was beating a mile a minute.

Then slowly she began to chant, "Uncle John, Uncle John, where are you?" I heard the car start up outside and pull off. I was alone with a little Gypsy chanting, "Uncle John." After a few more chants she stopped and all was quiet, too quiet.

Then I heard a low, husky voice, "This is Uncle John, what do you want?" A spotlight above the little Gypsy shown down on her and she began to jump up and down, joyfully, laughing at the top of her voice.

"It's Uncle John," she cried. "It's Uncle John." Immediately she began running toward me, jumping up and down, hair flying in every direction, screaming with joy, "It's Uncle John, I heard Uncle John!"

Trapped on the couch and terrified by this hideous monster coming nearer by the second. I jumped up and hit the little Gypsy woman, knocking her over a chair. I dashed out the door and ran all the way back to the dorm. Many have asked why I hit the little Gypsy and my only answer is that Dad said, "Son, in life always try to hit a happy medium."

After telling this story at camps, I often heard midnight calls of, "Uncle John, Uncle John where are you?" Once during our 1976 furlough when I worked with Alabama Baptist State Convention as Missionary in Residence in the Men and Boy's department with Mac Johnson and Jim Bethea, I led a church building team to Peru. One night after dinner we gathered around a swimming pool swapping stories. I told the Happy Medium story and when I finished someone shouted, "Throw him in the swimming pool." I ran for my life, barely escaping another baptism.

March 1956, a couple of weeks before our graduation, Ken Glass and I were asked to share some of our experiences and vast wisdom with the BSU undergraduates. Ken chose to share some of my army stories highlighting my two Basic Training experiences. He ended by saying, Jim went in the army as a Private and came out a Private which proves one thing: Jim is consistent." Ken became Director of State Missions with Virginia Baptist but unfortunately died at a young age. His sense of humor and love for life is missed.

I attended some sports events that year at Auburn, including a few baseball games but never had the desire to return to my past life in search of fame and fortune on the ball diamond. April 14, 1956 was a great day for my parents and me when I walked across the stage at A.P. I, now

Auburn University, to receive my diploma. Many thought it would never happen but with God, all is possible. Many others played a part in me reaching that memorable day. J.C. and Kathryn Oliver, my beloved parents, should have walked across the stage with me. Their prayers, patience and loving care will always be remembered. Thanks Mom and Dad!

Chapter 8

Ohio Mission

I applied for summer mission work after my graduation and was appointed to serve in the state of Ohio where Southern Baptist work was just beginning. I was assigned to an area that covered Northwestern Ohio, part of Pennsylvania and New York state. The missionary for that area was a dynamic young man named Paul Nevels whose main responsibility was starting churches in these areas. His wife Daisy, supported him doing all the wifely chores of a missionary mate.

After a couple of days of orientation in Columbus, four young missionaries, Daphne Ellis from Florida, Johnny Goodwin of Mississippi, Jo Strickland and I from Alabama, traveled with Paul and Daisy to their home in Cleveland. We didn't stay in Cleveland long enough to unpack our bags.

Our first job was in Willoughby, Ohio where our task was to strengthen a church where Alabamian Bob Hall was pastor and help start a new mission in the same city. Our work schedule began after breakfast at 9:00 for Vacation Bible School that ended at noon. Lunch was eaten on the field and consisted of a bologna sandwich and soft drink, and on special days, a nickel bag of potato chips. At 1:00 we began house–to–house survey of the neighborhood looking for prospects for the new Mission. At 5:00 we had dinner and returned to Bob Hall's church for a two–week revival. Around 10:00 p.m. we four collapsed in bed exhausted.

At the end of two weeks we celebrated a commencement service of Vacation Bible School. Our meeting place was over a raucous bar that had been quiet during the day. Paul asked me to give a brief message at the close of the service and an evangelistic invitation. When it came my turn, I stood, with the floor shaking from the loud music below, and gave a brief message and invitation. As we sang, a ten–year–old boy stepped forward, making his public profession in Christ. It was a joyful night.

On the way back to Cleveland, Paul said, "You have worked hard and deserve a day off. What do you want to do?"

I spoke up quickly saying, "The New York Yankees are playing the Cleveland Indians tomorrow and I would like to see the game."

Paul was excited and said, "I can get us tickets for a dollar apiece. Who wants to go?" We all volunteered.

After Daisy's exceptional breakfast, we left for the stadium early to see batting practice. This was the year Mickey Mantle was supposed to break Babe Ruth's home run record so the stadium was packed. We bought some peanuts and found our dollar seats located down the left field line. In the third inning, Mantle came to bat hitting right handed against a left handed pitcher and on the first pitch, hit a fast ball that rose high before us toward the left field fence. It was gone, over the fence with room to spare. Everyone, including the Indian fans, stood and a loud roar erupted that might have awakened the Bambino from his grave. We all believed we had seen history in the making, one of more than sixty home runs in the year for Mickey even though it didn't happen.

As Mantle trotted around the bases, a thought came to me. "Jim, what if you had stayed in baseball and by some miracle had made it to the big leagues and by another miracle that was you running around the bases. Would you exchange places with Mantle if you could?" Immediately, I remembered the night before when a young boy in a store front building, over a bar, made his decision to follow Christ as Captain of his life.

My answer was, "No, I wouldn't swap places with anyone on the field." Soon they would be in the crowd with us and what they accomplished would be very insignificant compared to the eternal destination and abundant life of a ten–year–old boy. It's true there are professional athletes, both men and women, called to this vocation and serve Christ and live by His Word. They have a strong testimony for the gospel and it's easy to see their career is not first priority, but the Savior they serve. However, sports wasn't my calling.

The ten–week mission experience in Ohio was inspirational and educational. After returning home I was asked to speak at church in Highland Gardens and when I arrived it was surprising to see a full house waiting to hear about our mission work and the spiritual needs of Ohio. The church gave me a generous love offering and I prepared to leave home to begin my studies at Southern Baptist Theological Seminary in Louisville, Kentucky.

Chapter

9

Southern Seminary

In The Fall of 1956 I enrolled in the School of Religious Education at Southern Baptist Theological Seminary, preparing to become a Baptist Student Union Director. There are differences in life on the campus of state school than at a Christian institution. I had much to learn coming from Auburn; enter Bob Franklin, a new friend from Howard Baptist College.

My new friend, Bob, asked me to attend church with him the first week we met and immediately after the sermon, he went forward and joined the church. I was under the impression you visited several churches before making your decision but Bob must have known something I didn't know. He did know something (or someone) I was unaware of, the professor of Children's work at the seminary, Miss Polly Hargis who was also the Children's Director at the church. I found out later Bob had made arrangements to be her assistant in the church nursery and we all know who made the best grades in Children's work at the seminary? Bob, of course.

During that first year I also learned Bob enjoyed playing Rook. I was visiting in his room one day when he challenged me to a game. He and I chose partners. My partner and I were close to winning with 460 points and Bob and his partner had less than a hundred. My partner left saying he had to study and I could coast out. The first hand, my new partner out bid his hand and we went set. Thinking he could atone for his sin he over bid again and now we had less than a hundred points and they were ahead by four hundred. The next hand they won the game and I was a "little upset." I grabbed the cards and threw them in the air. Bob, glaring at me, said, "Pick'em up."

I said, "I'm not going to pick'em up."

The other two players left the room. Bob standing at the door haughty gave the command, "Pick up the cards."

My answer. "I'll never pick the cards up."

Bob grabbed me around the neck, wrestled me to the floor and said, "I'll help you pick'em up."

I weighed more than Bob and had two courses in basic training in the army so I thought I could handle him easily. What I didn't realized was fat on me was muscle on Bob. Up and down we scuffled, landing hard on his roommate's bed, breaking it to the floor. I remembered my scissor hold, a strategy that seldom failed, and when I got my legs around his body I knew I had him. Squeezing hard I said, "Say Uncle." He said nothing, not even a grunt. Again I squeezed but still no results. Finally, with every ounce of strength, I gave it all I had, but no "Uncle" came forth.

Now the war took a turn for the worse for me. My strength had been depleted on a false maneuver and Bob had the advantage. Somehow he got my mouth and nose against his chest so tight I couldn't breathe. Pressing with all his might, he said, "Say Uncle."

Just before the lights went out, I whispered, "Uncle." I picked up the cards and went to my room.

Two weeks later, Bob and I were still good friends and I was again in his room: I have no idea why we were never in my room. "Let's go out on a double date," he said.

We called the girls and I asked Bob if he planned to wear a tie and he said no. After getting ready I went back to his room as usual and found Bob dressed and wearing a tie. I said, "I thought we weren't going to wear a tie."

"I changed my mind."

"I don't have one on, so why don't you take your's off?"

"No," he answered. "Go put one on."

"Now I was feeling I had just lost another Rook game and again I said with more emotion. "I'm not going to put one on. Take your's off."

"I'm not taking it off."

"Then I'll help you." I grabbed his tie and around and around we went again. We mopped up the floor with our clean clothes and his poor old roommate's bed went down again. However, this was my year. No more scissor holds depleting my strength, just good old GI hand–to–hand combat that seldom fails. I soon worked him into a similar hold that he used on me and he couldn't breathe. After three requests of "Say Uncle," Bob finally relented and I won. He didn't have to take his tie off, I had helped him with that and the dates were cancelled. We were too tired and dirty.

My seminary years were educational and inspirational. I sat under well trained and dedicated professors such as Findley B. Edge (Teaching For Results), Clyde T. Francisco (Major and Minor Prophets), Prof. Johnson (Speech) and J. Morris Ashcraft (New Testament). During those years thirteen professors rebelled against the president of the seminary, Duke McCall over personality conflicts. One recanted but the other twelve didn't and were dismissed. Several of those twelve were good professors but were fired because of their rebellion.

My church work during the seminary years was Minister of Music and Youth at Franklin Street Baptist Church located in a poor section of Louisville, named the Hay Market. My first summer in Louisville, I had the great privilege of serving with an energetic Royal Ambassador leader from Kentucky named J.C. Ballew. J.C.'s heart was to lead boys to Christ and teach them how to swim. I helped enlist and train camp counselors, then worked six weeks at Camp Cedermore near Shelbyville, Kentucky and Clear Creek Baptist School in Pineville. I fell in love with Royal

Ambassador work and thought that might be my calling, but it wasn't to be. God had another plan.

Bob and I graduated together in 1958 with Masters Degrees in Religious Education and I remained at the seminary another year working on the Bachelor's of Divinity degree.

One of my baseball buddies from Montgomery, Cary Harden, graduated with us and was looking for a church. He knew I had worked in Ohio and asked if I could help him find a church there. I called Paul Nevels and soon Cary was on his way to Cleveland. He and his wife, Mary Jo and daughters, served faithfully in Ohio for many years but Cary was called home to the Lord at a young age. Mary Jo and family still live and serve in Ohio.

After the summer's work with J.C., I still had three weeks free before classes began. I wrote Glorieta Baptist Assembly in New Mexico and applied for a staff position and was accepted. Little did I expect the life – changing experience that lay ahead.

[illegible] and I [illegible] might that night be in my college, but I wanted to be [illegible] God had another plan.

Robert [illegible] married [illegible] in 1958 and [illegible] children [illegible] Mother [illegible] and [illegible] at [illegible] [illegible] grave [illegible] on the [illegible] of [illegible] [illegible]es.

One of the baseball buddies from [illegible] Montgomery, [illegible] He later [illegible] with [illegible] was a long [illegible] church. He saw I had worked in Ohio but [illegible] I could help him find a church then. [illegible] Paul [illegible] Cal was on his way to Cleveland. He and [illegible] and daughter served a family in Ohio for many years [illegible] was called home to the Lord [illegible] and family still live and serve in Ohio.

[illegible] three weeks [illegible] I went [illegible] Barron Assembly in [illegible] and applied [illegible] position and was accepted [illegible] change [illegible] experience that [illegible] ahead.

Chapter 10

Love Blossoms

My trip out West was very unusual from the beginning. I joined up with some Alabama guys going to Glorieta with one purpose in mind, beating the Glorieta staff softball team. The leader of the team had worked six weeks at Glorieta but upon leaving promised his old team mates he would return with some players and teach them how to really play softball. I was drafted on the team when they learned I could play.

The Alabama guys were a "little" loco en la cabeza (crazy in the head) from the start. There were two car loads of us and their favorite pastime was dropping firecrackers out the car window hoping they would explode under the other car following them. While traveling in the second car I knew a firecracker would explode under us, igniting the gas tank and sending us into outer space like a rocket. At one stop, they bought Mexican peppers and smeared them on the hand of one of the boys hoping to see it burn every part of his body he touched, beginning with his eyes.

By the grace of God I made it to Glorieta in one piece and with no serious body burns. My job was working in the mess hall and I found out my boss was the staff softball coach. Every time I requested time off to play with the Alabama team I was denied. I finally got the message that if I were to play at all it had to be on the staff team. I became very unpopular with the Alabama boys the first day I showed up playing with the staff.

We, the staff, never lost a game to the Alabama team and in one game I got a good hit over the center fielder's head, scoring a couple of runs. I was surprised when the pitcher approached me with a dim sparkle in his eye and said, "You were lucky to hit that pitch." The Alabama team returned home defeated and as far as I know didn't blow themselves up along the way.

Not long after the "mini-world series" was over I skinned my knee playing in another game and was told I should see the nurse for first–aid. I was expecting to find an older woman but instead I met this young, good looking girl named Marilyn White who was a recent graduate from the University of Oklahoma. We talked as she treated me and discovered we both had been at the 1953 student meeting in Glorieta. For the remainder of the week I returned to the infirmary for "treatment" by nurse White and the young Oklahoma girl became more interesting to me every day. Each time I saw her I had strange feelings something was happening inside of me I couldn't explain. After one visit I asked to sit with her me in the Sunday evening worship service but she said she was sitting with someone else. My heart fell but later I breathed a sigh of relief when I saw her sitting by a girlfriend and not a boy.

After the service I "accidentally" met her. "Can I walk you to the dorm?" I asked. She consented. After leaving the auditorium we stepped out on the porch that was usually filled with people but to our surprise we were alone. We stopped, I looked into her eyes and holding her close, we kissed. No one told me there were to be fireworks that night, but there were, along with thunder, lightning and fog horns though there was no fog. I was smitten from head to toe.

Finally, composing myself, we walked to her dorm and along the way I learned Marilyn had the same desire I had for missions. Before leaving we prayed together. Though born many miles apart I believed God had brought us together. Walter Porter, an ex–roommate at Auburn, was at Glorieta and later I heard he put in a good word for me.

The week was over all too soon and I had to return to the seminary and Marilyn went to the University of Colorado to work on a master's degree in nursing. After returning to the seminary I read and re-read all the letters I received from Colorado. At Thanksgiving I visited Marilyn and her family in Tulsa and proposed marriage to her. She accepted.

At Christmas she visited me and my family in Montgomery and we announced our marriage plans.

February 28, 1958 Marilyn Jean White and I were married in holy matrimony at the First Baptist Church, Tulsa Oklahoma, Dr. Warren Hultgren officiating. Our honeymoon was the trip back to the seminary in Louisville.

Our first home was a basement in an old seven-gabled house overlooking Cherokee Parkway, a noted historical and picturesque park in Louisville. Not many ventured out on those snowy, winter days in the park except a few boys pulling and pushing their snow toboggans up and down the little hills.

Marilyn got a job at the Kentucky Baptist Hospital and I continued my studies. After three months in our honeymoon apartment we moved to the Fuller Apartments on the seminary campus. It was during this time another ex-roommate, Napp Granade, enrolled in the seminary, bringing his wife Sarah and their four children with them. Marilyn and I spent many hours with the Granade family usually arriving around meal time.

Marilyn became pregnant and had to give up her job at the hospital but I was hired at a Firestone Tire Store in Louisville, selling and mounting tires and also playing Santa Claus at Christmas. It was at this store I bought a used television for $20 which followed us halfway round the world before it blew it's last fuse.

On November 30, 1958, two days after her birthday, Marilyn gave birth to our first child, a Kentucky Colonel named James Daniel. The remainder of our seminary days were very pleasant with visits from our parents, student friends and challenging seminary classes. At the end of the school year I was called to the First Baptist Church, Russellville, Alabama as Minister of Music and Director of Religious Education. My seminary buddy Bob Franklin, serving in Alabama, had recommended me.

Chapter 11

Two Missions: Alabama and Ohio

Marilyn, Danny and I moved to Russellville, Alabama June, 1959 and I began my first full time job under the supervision of pastor, Rev. J.O. Colley. My duties were to prepare and direct the church choir, lead congregational singing, and help the Sunday School grow. My first plan was to teach Findley B. Edge's book, *Teaching for Results.* My salary was one hundred dollars a week.

Rev. Colley outlined my schedule of work the first day. I was to be at work at 8:00 am, do all my office work until noon and take an hour off for lunch. From 1:00 until 5:00 pm I was to visit prospects and church members in need. I could have learned more from Rev. Colley if we had visited together sometimes, but it was not to be.

I had little formal education in church music but enjoyed selecting the specials, choir rehearsals and leading the worship services Sunday morning and evening. I also took pleasure in singing solos. At Auburn I had private voice lessons and sang in two operas. While in the Army I looked up the well-known music professor, Dr. Hawthorne, who taught me voice for a year and advised me to drop out of college and study with him fulltime making music my career. I never felt led in that direction.

Near the end of my first year in Russellville I realized my time was short at the church. A conflict arose between the pastor and me that was a combination of several things, which included my inexperience in church work and lack of maturity. I submitted my resignation and was given two week vacation.

Paul Nevels had visited us and told about Brook Park, a suburb of Cleveland, where 1,200 homes were being built each year with only one small Protestant church in the community. A Baptist witness was greatly needed and Paul asked us to pray about being the pastor in Brook Park. I often wonder how I was called as pastor of this important place of ministry.

It may have happened like this.

In heaven one day the Lord approached Paul, the Apostle, and said, "We need a church in Brook Park, Ohio. I'm appointing you as chairman of a pulpit committee to search out the man for this important work. When your committee finds the man report to me."

"Yes sir, Lord. I'll be glad to do it." said Paul.

Immediately Paul chose six men for the committee: Abraham, Apostles Peter and John, Moses, Charles Spurgeon, and Adoniram Judson and called them to order. "Gentlemen," he began. "The Lord has given us the task of finding a pastor for a new church to be started in Brook Park, Ohio."

Peter broke in and said, "How do you plan to find this man and what are the qualifications for this job?'

"One question at a time, Peter. Let's look first at the qualifications for this job. First, I believe he must have a firm theological education. Second, he will need preaching/pastoral experience and finally he must have been successful in his work. Each person you bring before this committee with these qualifications will be presented to the Lord for the call."

Immediately Spurgeon spoke up and said, "I believe I have just the man for the job. Ben lives in Florida and meets all the qualifications."

"We'll begin with him," said Paul. "Give his name to the Lord and he'll make the call."

There was no hesitation and Ben was approached by the Lord for the job. "Did you say Ohio?" asked Ben.

"Yes I did," said the Lord. "Brook Park, in the Cleveland, Ohio area. It is a growing community where there are many lost souls and only one small church trying to reach them."

Ben hesitated and finally said, "Lord, you know my wife and I are close to retirement and we've bought a lot near the Pensacola Beach where we hope to retire. There are many churches around Pensacola where I can continue to preach. Please have me excused."

After Jesus' report to the committee, Paul said, "We are back at square one. Any more suggestions?"

"As a matter of fact, said Moses, "I know a successful pastor in Georgia named Brandon who meets the qualifications and will do a good job."

"Great," said Paul. "Give his name to the Lord."

Again the Lord wasted no time contacting the new candidate. After all the job was thoroughly described to Brandon he said, "Lord, I just bought a new car, I mean a used car and I'm not sure it will make it that far. Ohio is very far from Georgia for a used car. Please have me excused."

After the committee got the Lord's report, Paul said, "Three strikes and we're out. Who's got the perfect candidate? This has got to be the one" Looking around the group, Paul said, "John, we haven't heard from you. Surely you know a man of love that will fill the place of service."

"Well, as a matter of fact I do know a loving pastor and he does meet the qualifications. His name is Tom, shall I give his name to the Lord?"

"By all means," repeated all the committee members.

Upon receiving the name, the Lord visited Tom, the loving pastor and gave the call. There was no hesitation in his answer. "I just got married. I'm not going."

The committee was getting nowhere and even Paul was getting a little discouraged. After a long silence in which all were engaged in prayer, Abraham said softly, "I know of a possibility but you might not accept him."

"Fire away," said Judson. "We're at the bottom of the barrel. He just might work."

"He's a young man serving in Russellville, Alabama at the present time. He's married and has one small child. His name is Jim."

"Well, does he have theological education?" asked Paul.

"Not exactly. He majored in Religious Education so he's limited in theology."

"What about preaching/pastoral experience?" asked Spurgeon.

"Not too good there either. He has preached a few times but has never been a pastor."

Quickly Paul answered, "That's not good. But I suppose he's been successful in his church work."

There was a long pause before Abraham answered. "Not exactly," he began. "He has just been asked to resign by the pastor."

Loudly Paul asked, "A moral problem?"

"Oh no, not at all. Looks like only a misunderstanding between he and the pastor."

For the first time the committee began chatting among them selves until finally Paul said, "Let's come to order. Do any of you have any questions for Abraham?" All were quiet.

Standing, Paul addressed Abraham, "Are you recommending this man for the Ohio job?"

"Yes I am mister president," came his reply.

Almost to himself Paul murmured, "I don't guess he can do a lot of damage in Ohio. I understand there won't be but around thirteen at the church to begin with." Clearing his throat he said, "Abraham has recommended Jim from Russellville, Alabama to be called to the First Baptist Church of Brook Park, Ohio. All in favor raise your hand. The motion carried four to three. The Lord was informed about the decision, Jim was contacted and accepted the call. The rest is history.

The question was how we were to make a living since the new church couldn't pay a salary. As a nurse, Marilyn could find work almost anywhere and usually made a good salary. However, from the birth of our first child to the last she stood on the principle her place was in the home, taking care of her husband and children and my place was the bread winner. I questioned that principle at times but always came back to her point of view. Though we had little money and no job in Cleveland, Marilyn never wavered in going to Ohio with me. Her love and faith kept us happy in our joint decisions during all our missionary career. How blessed I have been to have such a spiritually mature and loving mate.

The first of June, 1960, Marilyn, eighteen–month old Danny and I packed all our earthly goods and, with the help of cousin Artie Burnett, left the deep South and moved North. I shall never forget the deep emotion I felt as we crossed the Ohio River from Kentucky to Cincinnati. I thought of Abraham leaving home, seeking a land God had promised which wasn't a place of ease but nevertheless a place of untold blessings. So it would be for us.

We experienced culture shock when Marilyn entered a doughnut shop in Cleveland and after taking the order the waitress looked at Marilyn in amazement and asked, "Where are you from?"

Paul found us an upstairs apartment in the town of Berea, a city adjacent to Brook Park. Immediately we began visiting in our new field and made several key visits to prospects for the new church that was to begin in two weeks. Paul had named the mission the First Baptist Church of Brook Park and found a place to meet in the Elementary School.

The first Sunday service began on time with thirteen people present, seven adults and six children. Marilyn taught the children while I preached the sermon. At the end of the service I gave the invitation to become part of the church and said, "When I step around the pulpit it signifies Marilyn and I are joining the church." It was thrilling to see all the other adults make the decision to join on the first stanza. We remained after the service for prayer and plans for the church and were off and running.

The policy of the Home Mission Board of our Convention at that time was to help a new church only when it was ready to put their pastor on fulltime salary. They then gave the church $150 a month for six months, $100 for three months and $50 for the last three months. We were a long way from that help so I began searching for secular work. For five weeks I looked without success but our needs were always met and we knew we were in God's will.

My first job, selling Singer Sewing machines, lasted only one week. Then, by a miracle, I got a job in Brook Park at the Firestone Warehouse shipping merchandise to stores, one being where I had worked while a seminary student. I worked five days a week, eight hours a day and made a good salary. At the end of the year I was laid off along with several others and was approached by church members asking the salary needed if I went full time. I heard if a week's salary paid the month's rent, you could live on the other three week's salary. Our rent was eighty–seven dollars a month so my request was eighty-seven dollars a week and I was surprised it was granted. Now the Home Mission Board could help us with the year's supplement.

For two years our church prayed we could leave the Elementary School and move into our own building. We looked at lots in Brook Park and discovered the price was very high, much too high for our budget. A new church member, Clyde Macabee, discovered three acres across the street from Brook Park in Middleburg Heights for only nine thousand dollars. (later the church was renamed Park Heights Baptist) My home church in Alabama, Highland Gardens Baptist, helped set up a bond program for us and bought the first $10,000 bonds. This allowed us to buy the property and build the walls. Few in Ohio were familiar with church bonds and the six percent interest wasn't much incentive to buy them.

A recent summer missionary, Jerry Don Reynolds, sent us a thousand dollar check and two one hundred dollar bills in an envelope as a gift for our building fund. That gift was enough to finish the walls and build the roof. Money was scarce and much of the work on the building was done by voluntary labor, a few working late at night not to jeopardize their jobs as union employees. One morning, while putting in the cement floor, we were visited by a union official who wanted to see our contractor. The contractor was introduced, and the union official asked who installed our pluming. When told it was none of his business the union official hit our contractor and ran. As he passed me he yelled, "Your contractor hit me." It was obvious he was lying when we saw a big burse on Clyde's face.

That afternoon I called *The Cleveland Plain Dealer*, informed them what happened and a couple of days later a reporter and photographer arrived and recorded every detail. On November, 28th, Marilyn's birthday, a large article came out in the paper. They published a picture of our unfinished building with me holding a cross–cut saw. Two days later, on Danny's birthday, an editorial came out in the paper with the title, "Leave The Baptist Alone."

Two weeks later the local newspaper printed more details, including the name of the union official. These newspaper articles brought new members to our church along with cash gifts. That was the end of problems with Union Officials.

That year Highland Gardens Baptist Church sent their pastor, R.E. Mckee and Music Director Bill Collister and wife Ann to lead us in revival services. During that revival our second son, Joel David was born into the Oliver missionary family.

Chapter 12

Bond Sales

When we volunteers began building the rafters of the roof we didn't have a carpenter in the church. One of our engineers said he had worked it out on his slide rule each rafter needed twenty–seven nails in each corner. Later I heard about an unemployed carpenter who consented to work for us and when he arrived he was amazed at our work saying each rafter needed only five or six nails in the corners. To this day there are rafters in the building with twenty–seven nails in each corner.

Some church bonds matured in a year and others over a period of time but bills steadily increased and with the school rent we were fast getting into a financial bind. For weeks no bonds were sold, halting construction on the building. At Christmas, I asked the church for permission to return home hoping to sell more bonds. They granted me permission and on December 20th Marilyn, Danny, Davy and I left for Alabama. Back at home I visited churches, family and friends hoping to make some sales but had no success. One of my trips was to Alexander City, north of Montgomery. Separating the two cities is Lake Martin, a recreational haven for many, where I had spent many leisurely hours fishing, swimming and camping with my family. On the south side of the long bridge is a cabin where Hank Williams wrote his famous song, "Pore ol' Kaw–liga."

After an unsuccessful day of bond sales in Alex City, I headed home. As I drove onto the bridge I had the feeling someone was in the car with me. There was communication between us though not audible. It was strange I wasn't intimidated. The first was a question. "Look to your left Jim, and tell me, who lives on the lake?"

"My Uncle Norman and Aunt Nell."

Another question. "Anyone else?"

"Yes, my Uncle John Sebron and Aunt Martha."

"Do you enjoy being on the Lake with them?"

I answered, "Yes."

There was a brief silence and then, "Jim, I know you love this lake in the summer with your family, fishing and camping , but you can't do that living in cold Ohio. Your parents need you here and they deserve to be near you and their grandchildren. Your dad said he had a job for you so why don't you leave Ohio and return home? Your work is failing and the people aren't behind you and are not buying the bonds. Why don't you quit and return to Alabama?" I was alone again and left to ponder these thoughts.

Satan isn't omnipresent like God and since he can be in only one place at a time must depend on lesser demons to do his work, of which he has many. However, Satan does tempt us personally at times and I believe that night, crossing the Kowaliga Bridge, I had a real encounter with the Chief Tempter, Satan himself. God gave me the strength to resist his temptation and we returned to Ohio. Back in Ohio several church members approached me and said, "Brother Jim, since this is our church we should buy the bonds." They did buy enough to finish the building and God won the victory.

After the building was finished we lacked one thing before we could move in; approval of the septic tank pipe line by city officials. I helped our contractor lay the eighty–yard line from the building to the tank by the road and then we called the inspector. Our relationship with the city inspectors wasn't good since our contractor had openly disobeyed some of their rules. When the inspector arrived, he placed his level on the first pipe and said, "Failed." He fastened a red tag on the pipe and walked away. The next week my father-in-law was visiting us and helped me lay the line again. I called the inspector who placed his level on two pipes this time before saying, "Failed."

When he put his level on the pipes, I happened to see something interesting, a Masonic ring. I said to myself, "Mr.

Inspector, the next time you visit us you'll meet a member of our church who just happens to be a Mason."

I laid the line one more time, called the inspector after I called our Masonic member. The two men passed a sign or two (possibly my imagination) and the inspector laid his level on two pipes and then came the beautiful word, "Passed." Within a week we left the Elementary School and moved into our new building. On August 5, 1962, our son John Paul was born. We were now the proud parents of three wonderful, energetic sons.

A key Biblical promise I tried to live by in my ministry are the words of Jesus, "Follow me and I will make you fishers of men." One Tuesday night, a faithful member, Frank Suplita, and I visited a man in our community named Carlos. I had prepared a tract with scripture verses related to becoming a Christian with a picture of Jesus standing at the door knocking. Frank and I presented the gospel to Carlos and after prayer asked if he would like to follow Christ as his Savior. Almost in a shout, Carlos said, "No." Frank and I were shocked and didn't know what to do next. Finally we made our way to the door and were about to leave when Carlos said, "Well preacher, I guess you failed tonight."

I turned back to Carlos and asked, "What do you mean we failed?"

"Well, you came to win me but I wasn't won."

I looked him in the eyes and said, "We didn't fail tonight, Carlos. Probably this is first time you heard yourself say, you don't want Christ in your life. I don't believe you can live with that very long."

A couple of weeks later Carlos and his wife and children were in Sunday School and a week later attended the Sunday night service. At the invitation they came forward and gave their hearts to Christ and were baptized soon afterwards. It was no surprise when Carlos began preaching and later became a pastor. Years later, while on furlough, I preached in a church near Cleveland and told the story of Carlos. After the service a man said to me, "Brother Jim, thanks for witnessing to Carlos Browning because he won me to Christ." To God be the glory! A modern example of "fishers of men" is my ninety-two year old Uncle, John Sebron Oliver who is active every week in sharing his faith to the lost and sick. May many follow his example.

Chapter

13

Rule of The Day

WE HAD NOT been in our new building long before some members began talking about leaving the Southern Baptist Convention and become an Independent church. At a business meeting I said, "Becoming an Independent church isn't an option but I want to see the hands of those who want to leave the Southern Baptist Convention and become an Independent church." Five families raised their hands and nine families voted to remain in the convention. In only a few weeks, all five of the families that voted to become independent left the church, cutting deep into our outreach and finances. Once again I had to return to secular work.

I applied and was accepted by the Cleveland School Board of Education as a substitute teacher, and each morning I called the secretary who assigned the substitutes for the day and received my appointment. I made twenty dollars a day and worked five days a week and after receiving my one hundred dollar check I took it to our treasurer who then wrote out my salary check for one hundred dollars.

At one school I was asked to "teach" a wood–working class in which I had no training or experience. The principal, a retired Army captain, gave me a brief orientation saying since the job was new to me the activity of the day would be only sanding the project the students were working on. Then in his military manner, he said, "Mr. Oliver, there is one rule for the day, no electric saws will be turned on."

Everything went well for four periods but in the fifth a boy turned on an electric saw. I rushed over and turned it off. Ten minutes later he turned it on again but this time I didn't go immediately to him but only told him to turn it off. He didn't and almost immediately ran the blade into his finger. He was rushed to the hospital and I didn't see him again. The rule for substitutes was to check out at the secretary's office before leaving. I quietly entered the office, mumbled to the secretary I was going and hurried to the door. I thought I had made it but as I reached for the door knob, the secretary said, "Mr. Oliver, the principal wants to see you in his office."

As I stood at attention before the principal, he asked, "Mr. Oliver, what was the rule of the day?"

"Not allow any machine to be turned on."

"And what happened Mr. Oliver?"

"Well, when the machine was first turned on I immediately had it turned off, but the second time I only told the boy to turn it off."

The ex–captain exploded. "Mr. Oliver, you don't tell these kids to do anything, you make them do it." I was a little surprised how quickly he recovered. "Mr. Oliver these things happen and the boy is fine and if you have the opportunity to return, you will be welcomed." I left wounded but somewhat encouraged.

A couple of weeks later I received another call from a different school as substitute for another shop class. Students used electric saws to cut plastic cubes to make table lamps. When reporting to the class, the principal said he realized I knew very little about this work and a trained teacher had been called to take my place the next day. In the first class I told the pupils I knew less of what they were doing than they did, but I was in charge and the rule of the day was that no machines would be turned on. If they didn't obey, off to the office they go. What I didn't know was the principal was in the storage room behind me and heard what I said. He came rushing out of the room and I thought I might not make it through the day. However, at the end of the day the principal called me into his office and said, "Mr. Oliver, I called our department and told them not to send another teacher, we had our man. You will return, won't you?" I was happily surprised and said yes. The regular teacher was seriously ill and I was asked to remaine as the substitute for the rest of the school year.

On the last day of school, the director of the Manual Shop Division of Cleveland schools was introduced to me. He asked if I would be willing to teach in his department. He said I could take summer classes and attend evening classes while teaching until I was fully qualified. I was honored but said I couldn't comply.

Earlier in the year the director of the Social Welfare Department of Cleveland heard I had a degree in Sociology and offered me a job as a Social Case Worker but I knew neither of these opportunities were God's will for Marilyn and me. Foreign missions was on the horizon.

Chapter 14

Welcome Aboard

Each year it was a custom at our church to have a two-week revival and I heard Don Heiss, a furloughing missionary from Japan, was available. I wrote asking if he would be our evangelist and he consented. The revival services were very inspirational as well as helping Marilyn and me learn more about the procedure of becoming missionaries.

After the services, we corresponded with the Foreign Mission Board about our interest and call to missions. The response of the board was although I had a seminary degree, Masters of Religious Education, I did not have sufficient experience in that field. I had enough experience as a pastor but didn't have the pastor's degree, Bachelor's of Divinity. Therefore, I would need more experience in religious education or the pastor's degree.

One day, Bill Slagle, our new area missionary, said, "Dr. Cal Guy, mission professor at Southwestern Baptist Theological Seminary in Ft. Worth, Texas, is an excellent teacher to study under for a missionary career." We prayed and decided my call was primarily preaching so I applied at Southwestern and was accepted.

Marilyn was now expecting the birth of our fourth child. I had been reading about Adoniram Judson, the first foreign missionary from the United States and was very impressed by his life. I said to Marilyn, "If our fourth child is a boy, we must name him Adoniram."

She said, "If you named him Adoniram I will call him A don aram." A beautiful girl, Jean Elizabeth, came into the Oliver family solving the name problem. Only a few months after Jeannie's birth I did a very difficult thing; I resigned from the First Baptist Church of Brook Park, Ohio. I wept remembering every member that joined the church and the victories God had given us during four years as pastor. At the time of my resignation, the church owed me three hundred dollars back salary. Some members borrowed five hundred dollars from the bank, gave us three hundred for back salary and two hundred vacation pay. Our move to Ft. Worth, Texas cost five hundred dollars almost to the penny.

At Ft. Worth I enrolled at the seminary in the summer, my favorite time in school, and Marilyn got a job at All

Saints Hospital. I wrote the Board saying I was enrolled in the seminary and lacked only one year before graduating and then could be appointed. They responded they didn't appoint anyone directly from the seminary, I needed to pastor a church. Immediately I ran to my professor of preaching and told him my dilemma and that weekend he called saying a church named Red Springs Baptist, about three hours from Ft. Worth, was looking for a pastor. That Sunday all six of us traveled to Red Springs, Texas where I preached both services and was called as pastor. Marilyn resigned her job at All Saints Hospital and we moved to the church pastorium in Red Springs. Again I wrote the Board saying I had a church and would be ready for appointment in a year and they responded they never appointed anyone out of a church unless they had been there at least two years. I finished my seminary studies at Southwestern in one year and had another year to serve at Red Springs.

At the seminary I took every missions course Dr. Guy taught and was greatly influenced by his knowledge and enthusiasm for foreign missions. Other outstanding classes at Southwestern were Ethics by Dr. William Pinson, Jr.; Dr. Hubert Drumwright, the Book of Hebrews; Dr. John P. Newport, Philosophy of Religion; Dr. Curtis Vaughn, Greek New Testament; Dr. Jesse Northcutt, Preaching; and Dr. Yandall Woodfin, Theology. I was blessed by great professors in two Baptist seminaries.

One important contact I made at the seminary was an ex–pastor of Red Springs Baptist Church, Dr. Keith Parks, a furloughing missionary from the Philippines. Visiting him one day he pointed at me and said to a friend, "There's a man who will be appointed a missionary." When asked why, he said, "Because he's the pastor of Red Springs Baptist Church."

We were fortunate to have Dr. Parks one Sunday as our preacher and not many, if any, will forget his sermon, "Let My People Go." When he finished there wasn't a dry eye in the house and if ever we were ready to go to the mission field, it was then. A few years later Dr. Parks was elected president of the Foreign Mission Board and served with honor and distinction.

The first year at Red Springs, I preached both Sunday services and traveled to the seminary early Tuesday morning and had classes until Friday afternoon. Marilyn remained at Red Springs with Danny in the first grade and the other three at home. Sometimes, upon returning from the seminary, I saw Marilyn sitting on the front porch waiting for a long-lost husband from what some seminary wives called the men's vacation. Seeing her I knew immediately it was time to take her and the family out to eat in Seymour.

Red Springs, Texas was very different from Cleveland, Ohio. First there were no large buildings towering over us and you could see open land for miles and miles out the back door. Second, conversations were different; I would say, "The weather's good."

They answered, "If we don't get rain, the crops will die."

I said, "It sure was good to get rain."

They said, "If it doesn't stop soon, the crops will rot in the field." It took a year to learn the language.

Welcome Aboard

MEMOIR

After my seminary graduation, I had another year at the church. One of our members, Deacon Burkhalter, approached me one day and said, "Brother Jim, we know you can visit all the members and prospects of the church in a couple of days but what we need more than a full–time pastor are farm hands. If the church approves, will you work for me?"

I agreed and so did the church. My job was planting wheat and helping Brother Burkhalter strip cotton. The work was rewarding and provided extra income for our family. Close to the end of our second year at the church, I came in from the field tired and thirsty one hot, summer day and slumped into a chair in the kitchen waiting for supper.

The phone rang and at the other end came, "Is this Jim Oliver?"

"Yes," I answered.

"This is Sammy DeBoard of the Foreign Mission Board. Do you still want to be a missionary?"

"More than ever before," I said.

And then came the beautiful words, "Welcome aboard." We had made it! Our lives would be forever changed, rewarded and greatly blessed. We gave thanks to God.

Chapter

15

Language School

July, 1966 Marilyn and I traveled to Richmond, Virginia for our appointment and a two–week orientation on the campus of the University of Richmond. Both mom and dad were present at our appointment service and the children were well taken care of by members of the church at Red Springs. We, along with eighteen other couples and one single man, were appointed in a moving service by Dr. Baker James Cauthen who addressed each appointee by name, challenging us to give our best in the work where the Lord had called us.

After orientation we returned to Red Springs, resigned from the church and packed for our first assignment,

Language School, San Jose, Costa Rica. After saying farewell to church members, family and friends, Marilyn, Danny, Davy, Johnny, Jeannie and I boarded a plane in Miami and with ten other missionary couples flew to San Jose, Costa Rica. We were met in San Jose by other missionaries who were assigned as our "Big Brothers and Sisters." Our "Brother," Richard Clement and "Sister," Barbara helped us get established and familiarized to our new country and culture.

Costa Rica is a beautiful Central American country between Nicaragua and Panama, a land of lush jungles, playful monkeys, languid sloths, exotic birds and butterflies. The people are friendly and Costa Rica is the only Latin American country without an army. Veteran missionaries Sidney Goldfinch and wife Frances stood by our side when interpreters were needed and also provided social outings for our family. Sidney also took us on mission trips in Costa Rica during school breaks. Our school schedule was from eight until noon, five days a week, and afternoons for study and practice. Each family attended a local Baptist church on Sunday but couldn't understand much of the sermon.

The boys attended school, but Jeannie at three, was in the nursery. One day a boy threw a wooden block across the room, striking her just above the eye. The gash wasn't deep but required five stitches to close. As Jeannie recuperated I had some very unpleasant thoughts. Why did this boy hit Jeannie? The thought came to me it wasn't an accident but something planned. Something within me, the devil, suggested the boy's father was to blame and had to be confronted. A couple of days later I picked Jeannie up at the nursery and someone told me the father of the boy that hit Jeannie was there. Looking around I saw him, a huge man that looked as if he could play linebacker for the Dallas Cowboys football team. Something inside me said, "Wait, don't be too hasty to take revenge." When he recognized me he rushed over and began apologizing, saying he would pay the doctor bill. I said, "Not to worry, it wasn't that bad. We will pay the bill." He was very nice and so was I.

Language school wasn't all work and no play. Once Costa Rica missionary Don Doyle invited some of us to go fishing. His field of service was close to the Pacific Coast near the Province of Guanacasta and after a few hours drive we arrived at Playa de Coco (Coconut Beach), rented a cabin and prepared for our fishing trip. The sandy beach was grayish brown and the tide remained quiet and low. Surrounded by steep cliffs and hills, the horseshoe-shaped bay was an ideal place to relax and enjoy God's beautiful creation.

Don had made arrangements with a local fisherman to take us out in his home–made boat, so around three in the afternoon we made our first fishing trip. Farther out you could catch tarpon, snook, mahi–mahi, tuna and roster fish, just to name a few. Closer to the beach we caught our limit of yellow fin tuna. That night we were served a memorable dinner of shrimp and tuna.

Before going to bed we put on our bathing suits and went swimming in the warm Pacific and around midnight were floating high on small waves and down again touching our bare feet on the smooth sand below. Up and down we bobbled. I couldn't help saying, "Don't we feel sorry for all those back home who feel sorry for the poor missionaries."

Learning a new language is like becoming a child again, making many mistakes. One missionary progressed rapidly in learning Spanish and was asked to speak to a large group of women in the church. His theme was the importance of your interior life – *su vida interior*. He began hoping to say, "God is interested in your inner life," but instead said, "God is interested in your *su ropa interior*." (your underwear) It got worse as he continued. "God wants you to have clean underwear and give directions how to clean it."

For emphasis he slowly repeated this several times. The leader, trying hard to be polite and stifle the crowd, could contain herself no longer. All burst out in laughter.

It was a challenge to learn the language but rewarding when you could, as they say, "Defend yourself." Our year of language school was soon over and now we were excited to move on to Colombia, our adopted land.

Newlyweds

Off to Sunday School
Barranquilla,
Colombia

Kathryn, Jimmy,
J.C. Oliver

Oliver and Zokan Family. Row 1 Marilyn, Jim, Olivia Zokan, Addison, and Luke Oliver. **Row 2** John, Caleb, Joe, Aria and Karin Oliver. **Row 3** Chris, Natalie and Jeannie Zokan, Dan, Michele and Dave Oliver

Jim and Marilyn.
Barranquilla, Colombia

Happy School Days.
Barranquilla, Colombia

Pastor Jim, New Church, Parks Heights, Ohio

50 Years Later, Park Heights, Ohio

Pastor Jim F.B.C.
San Andres, Colombia

Colombia Missionaries and family

Jim and Fireman Crew Fort Benning, Georgia

Fireman Jim and New Trainee

Private Oliver

Amazon Trip Tony Docal, Dan, Dave, John Oliver, Kirk Schlup

A Bunch of Birds Mike's Motel
Leticia, Colombia

Center of the World
Near Quito, Ecuador

Dan and Mike Tsalickis
Leticia, Colombia

Temple Dedication
León del Medio,
Colombia

Sunday School
San Andres, Colombia

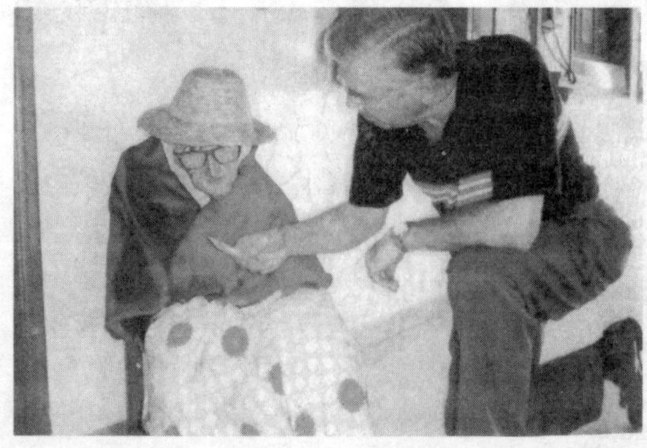

Personal Witnessing

Guajira Indian and Goats

Christ, The Only Hope
Evangelism Team

Royal Ambassadors and Leaders
San Andres, Colombia

Country Home in Colombia

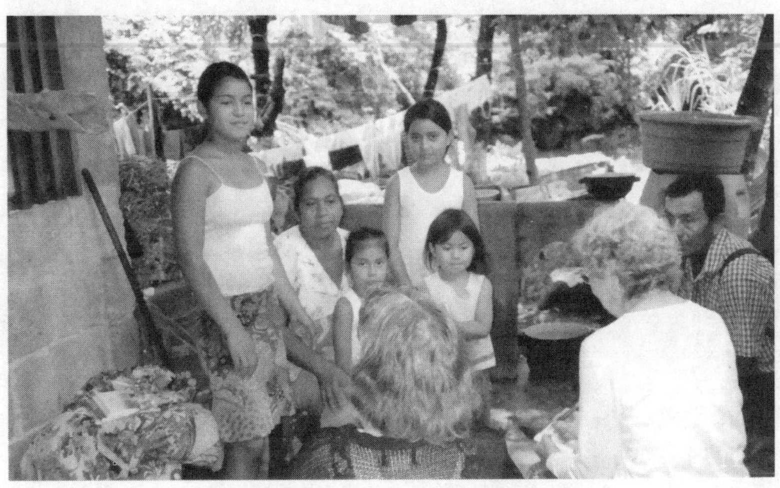

Marilyn Sharing the Gospel Near Cartagena, Colombia

Chapter

16

On To Colombia

BEFORE WE MOVED to our new mission field we returned to the States, crated our few worldly goods and had them transported to Miami where they were placed on the ship sailing to Cartagena. We bid farewell to church members, mom and dad White, and drove to Alabama, our last stop. We spent a couple of days with mom and dad Oliver at my Uncle Seb's cabin on lake Martin. Mother heated some water for dad's sprained foot and placed it close to the refrigerator to cool. Jeannie, age two, opened the refrigerator door and fell back into the scalding water. Immediately Marilyn and I rushed her to the hospital in Tallassee.

The next morning I called the Foreign Mission Board and informed them of the accident and our travel plans were postponed. Marilyn stayed with Jeannie every day in the hospital and nursed her back to health. My grandmother lived with my Aunt Nell in Tallassee but there was also room enough for the six Olivers. The boys enrolled in Tallassee schools as we patiently waited for Jeannie's recovery. When the doctors gave us the green light to travel with Jeannie, we informed the Board and were given the last week of November as our new traveling date. We said goodbye to all, flew to New York, saw Macy's Thanksgiving Parade and on November 26, 1966 boarded the *Santa Magdalena* Cruise Ship sailing to Cartagena, Colombia.

The five days aboard the *Santa Magdalena*, except for one rough day, was like a dream vacation. During the day we relaxed in the deck chairs in the warm sun, swam in the pool and met ourselves going and coming to the dining hall. In the evening we saw stellar movies and ate again. One meal was served on deck where we were introduced to South America fruits: mango, papaya, zapote, guanabana juice and more.

We arrival in Cartagena on November 30, Danny's ninth birthday. Marilyn had celebrated her thirty–third birthday on ship two days earlier. Our introduction to Colombia was Cartagena, a unique historical city where Spanish Conquistadores made their first sea port in the new land. We were met by veteran missionaries Helen Meredith of Cartagena and Dr. Jim and Esther Morris of Barranquilla. After brief introductions we loaded our carry–on luggage in Dr. Morris' truck and began the three hour trip to our new home.

I was assigned to two departments, Atlantico and Magdalena. Barranquilla, a city of 800,000 inhabitants, an important sea port ten miles up the Magdalena River from the Caribbean Sea and was the largest city in the Atlantico Department. The largest city in the Department of Magdalena was Santa Marta, a beautiful capital surrounded by Caribbean beaches making it a popular vacation resort for both Colombians and Venezuelan neighbors since accommodations were inexpensive and the beaches were safe for all ages. There were nine Baptist churches in Barranquilla and one in Santa Marta.

After one night with the Morris family we moved into the home of Dr. Glenn and Ila Breeden who were on furlough in Texas. It was here an American Exchange student, Ellis Leagans, visited us and became a lifelong acquaintance. After returning to the States he finished college and the seminary and along with his new bride Judy, was appointed to Colombia as missionaries. Today, Ellis is a key leader among missionaries in Central America. Other missionaries in Barranquilla at that time were Dean, B.J. Duke and Arlene Rogers, a single nurse working at the Baptist Clinic. Our first assignment was to hire a Spanish tutor to continue our language study.

Marilyn and the children attended Sunday School and worship at Central Baptist, Rev. Sebastian Barrios pastor, and played the piano for the worship services. Danny made his profession of faith and was baptized by Brother Barrios.

I made the rounds getting to know the Baptist Churches in Barranquilla. After several months on the field I preached my first sermon in Spanish and as far as I know it turned out, as they say in Spanish, *"Muy regular,"* which is a polite way of saying, not so hot. I don't believe that sermon was recorded in the historical archives of the Colombian Baptist Convention.

My first work in Barranquilla was with Horeb Mission. A Baptist layman, Ernesto Mesa, bought a piece of property in Barranquilla where he built his home and a mission. The pastor of the mission was a converted priest and the church grew under his and Ernesto's leadership with a small contribution from me. One day I was asked by a Clinic doctor, "Where are you serving."

I said, "Horeb Mission."

To my surprise his answer was, "That's like pumping formaldehyde into a dead body." Not very encouraging.

A few months later Ernesto Mesa suffered a financial reversal and lost his property, home and the mission building. It looked as if the doctor might be right. However, the mature Christians of the mission knew the church wasn't a building and the little congregation moved into rental property nearby. The mission soon became a church, called two seminary graduates, Rev. Alejandro Pajaro and wife Victoria as pastor and pianist and the church grew rapidly.

A few years later Dr. Robert Edwards and wife Dolores were appointed to serve at the Baptist Clinic. They joined Horeb Baptist Church and Robert became Sunday School teacher and music director and Dolores pianist. The Edwards served thirty-three distinguished years in the Barranquilla Clinic and upon retiring received well-deserved commendations from medical, civic and religious leaders of Colombia.

After furlough, Dr. Glenn and Ila Breeden, and their five sons, returned to their Barranquilla home. The Morris family resigned for medical reasons and returned to the States and we were assigned their house. The master bedroom of the house was up a small flight of stairs in the front, adjacent to the high–ceiling living room. The dining room was behind the living room and was served by the connecting kitchen. The two children's bedrooms were behind the living room, connected by a hallway.

It was in their bedrooms I found the children asleep during the night of the burglary. That night, after checking them, I stepped back into the hall and saw Marilyn coming down the stairs from the bedroom. Quickly I ran to her and held her tight. All was quiet. It became obvious no one was in our home but us and the present protection of the Lord. We reported the crime to the police but never heard anything more about the robbery.

Remembering the good work of J.C. Ballew with boys in Kentucky, we decided to start a Royal Ambassador Chapter not only to teach our boys but also reach their friends. We met Saturday mornings and studied world missions, memorized key scripture verses, participated in crafts and games but the most popular activity was camping trips. With the help of one of the boy's father, Fals Borda, we made a memorable trip into the highest mountain in Colombia, Sierra Nevada de Santa Marta. The top of the mountain, El Colon, is 19,029 feet and snow covered year–round. We didn't reach El Colon, and not even the snow, but we did get high enough where we thought we might freeze. No sleeping bag was able to keep us warm. National Geographic mountain climbers reached El Colon once and reported looked longingly down at the warm Caribbean beaches below as their toes were freezing. This was the setting of my third book, *Hootie In La Sierra Nevada de Santa Marta,* a book telling the story of the kidnapping of Chris' father.

The second year in Barranquilla we participated in an intensive evangelistic program called, La Campaña de Las Americas (The Campaign of The Americas). Several outstanding Latin and North American evangelists preached in our churches and open-air coliseums in and around the city. My job was to organize campaign prayer meetings, special visitation events and lead congregational singing in some meetings. During these revivals we saw great evangelistic response that helped existing churches grow and was an impetus to start new churches. Baptist laymen throughout Colombia participated in the Campaign to further the gospel in their native land. Simeon Gutierrez of Barranquilla and wife Lorraine provided housing for visiting evangelists and singers as well as obtaining permits for stadiums where services were held.

Among the missionaries living in Barranquilla there were three fishermen; Dr. Glenn Breeden, Jerry Ballard and me. Dr. Breeden and I were partners of a boat and motor that made trips to the Caribbean Sea and a large lake near Barranquilla. The real fisherman among us was the clinic prosthetic doctor, Jerald Ballard, a Louisiana native that I believed was born on the water. He built his own boat and fished lakes and rivers on his days off catching large tarpons and delicious snook.

Another missionary, Ross Thompson, who served in the Plains of Colombia (Los Llanos Orientales) fished with me once in Rio Frio (Cold River). Rio Frio flows into a large brackish lake named Cienaga Grande where many Colombians fish for a living. We trolled with a shiny, silver spoon and caught many hard fighting tarpon. We fished two days and it rained so hard one day I could hardly see Ross at the front of the boat.

After a couple of hours trolling up-river we came to a new motor boat tied to a dock in front of a modern home. Behind the house were several cars and many workers in the fields. As we got closer, a welled dressed man stepped off the porch and began walking toward us. I said, "Ross, I don't believe the fishing is better ahead. Why don't we turn around and go home." He agreed and we turned slowly and headed back to our car, looking over our shoulder now and then to see if we were followed by a powerful new motor boat.

During our fishing trip we discovered a city of homes built on rafts named Nueva Venice where many poor fishermen and families lived. Later we returned and donated clothing, food and Bibles. Very soon after our visit a new church was started by clinic employees on the beach near Nueva Venice.

We lived and worked as missionaries for almost thirty years in Colombia and came to know and experience her rivers, snowcapped mountains, white beaches, the fauna, and flora. This natural paradise also included rich coffee, oil, coal and green emeralds. It was a joy to work among such precious people surrounded by unfathomable natural beauty.

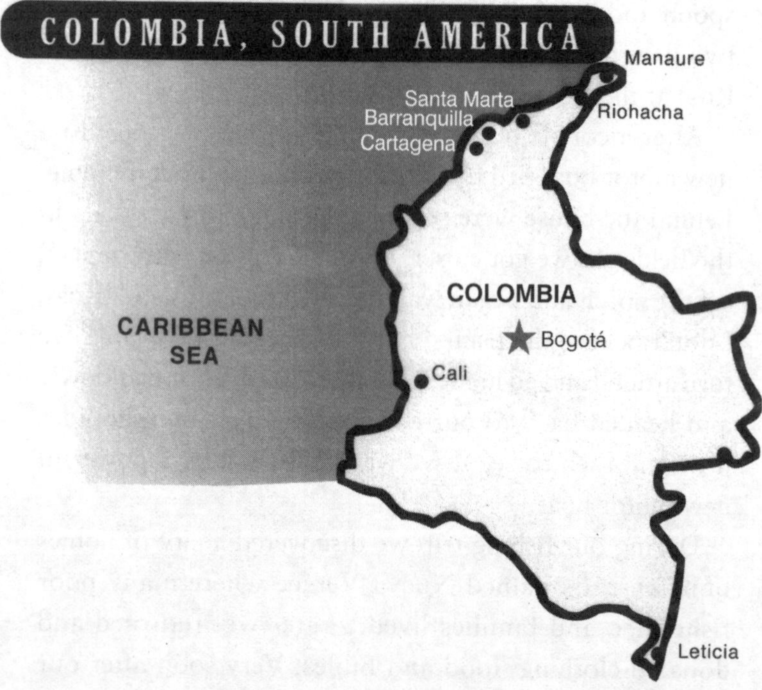

Chapter

17

Flight Lessons

IN JANUARY OF 1949, twenty-five acres were bought on the outskirts of the city of Cali by the Foreign Mission Board and the International Baptist Theological Seminary was born. Its purpose was to train men and women for Christian ministry. Students came from Central America and the five Bolivian countries of South America: Colombia, Venezuela, Bolivia, Peru and Ecuador. Professors of Theology, Religious Education and Music were appointed by the Mission Board. Miss Crea Ridenour was professor of Religious Education and a study of the seminary in 1970 revealed some pastors had a bias against Religious Education because it was taught only by women. Trustees made a search for a male professor to teach Religious Education and learned I had a Master's degree in that field. They asked if I would take the position and after prayer, Marilyn and I accepted the call and made plans to move to Cali after returning from furlough.

The policy of the Board was missionaries served four years on the field and returned to the States for a year's furlough. We returned to the States August, 1971 and after visits with our parents, I enrolled in Southwestern Baptist Theological Seminary for more preparation for teaching at the seminary in Cali. All four children were enrolled in school and Marilyn had the job of preparing meals, clothing and keeping us all on the right track.

Casually talking to a classmate one day I said, "Since I was a boy in the Civil Air Patrol in Montgomery, I have wanted to get a pilot's license."

The next day I received a telephone call. "Jim, this is Ralph Capshaw. I hear you are interested in getting a pilot's license. I'm certified as a flight instructor and can give you free ground school and flight training but you'll need to rent a plane. You can rent a Cessna 172 for a good price at the club where I'm a member."

I accepted his offer, rented a plane and began my flight training the next week. After several months of training, and solo flights, I was ready to complete the final test to receive my license; a solo flight to at least two cities a hundred miles from Meacham Field in Ft. Worth.

November 22 was scheduled for my flight. When I awoke it was cloudy and looked like it might rain. I called Ralph. "Doesn't look good does it."

"Not to worry," said Ralph. "I just called the airport and they gave the green light for you to make a VFR flight (Visual Flight Rules) and said it would be good experience for a student pilot." That turned out to be the understatement of the year.

I kissed Marilyn and the four kids goodbye and wondered if I would ever see them again. At the airport, I checked out the plane, buckled in and called, "Clear prop." I contacted ground control and was given the green light to taxi to the runway. As I lined up on the runway I heard, "Cessna 231, cleared for takeoff." My heart was beating as I sped down the runway and at the proper speed pulled the controls back and was airborne. Clearing the runway, I checked my compass for direction and climbed to the proper altitude.

My first stop was Seymour, Texas and arriving at the small airport I had a strong cross wind and couldn't land the first three times. The fourth time I set it down hard, very hard. A good friend, Rev. Don Chaffin, pastor of the First Baptist Church in Seymour, met me at the airport. We chatted and after a meal together, he signed my logbook and I was ready for my second leg of my cross country flight, Breckenridge, Texas.

The runway looked very long and my first thought was that half of the runway was enough for the takeoff but then decided I would use it all. I taxied the full length of the runway, turned around, revved the engine, let off the brakes and down the runway I went. My normal takeoff speed was ninety miles and hour but I was getting close to the end of the runway and the fence and was only going seventy miles an hour. Near the end of the runway, I pulled back the controls without looking at my speed and cleared the fence with a couple of feet to spare. Setting my compass again and climbing to the proper altitude I began humming, "O What A Beautiful Morning."

The beautiful morning and the song didn't last very long; it began to rain. It was a light rain at first but then it began coming down in sheets, making it impossible for me to see the propeller. The time for pilots without instrument training, like me, to stay airborne without any reference to the ground is short. I couldn't see ahead but thankfully I had side vision and had no trouble keeping the wings level and staying on course.

The rain didn't stop and finally the thought came, why don't I pray? I prayed, "Lord, let it stop raining." It did stop, and I was happy but then it started raining again. This time, I added something else. "Lord, let it stop raining but don't let it start again." Sure enough that prayer was answered also but in the place of rain came a strong head wind. It got so bad I believed the wings couldn't take any more so I had to make an emergency landing. Slowly I began to descend but the closer I got to the ground the more huge boulders I saw, all about three feet apart. If I did land it would probably be a crash landing and I might not survive. At that moment a verse of scripture came to mind. "What profit is there in my blood when I go down to the pit? Shall the dust praise thee?"

I knew I couldn't land, so slowly I began to ascend again and all of a sudden the clouds cleared and before me was a beautiful lake by my goal, Breckenridge, Texas. Praise God, success was in sight.

I circled the field at Breckenridge, checked the wind sock and put the nose directly into the wind and knew I had to land on the first try. I was successful and coming to a stop I felt I had been beaten by a large bamboo pole. I was so weak I could barely get out of the plane. After touching the wonderful solid ground I found a phone and called Meacham Field in Ft. Worth and was told the weather was bad and only IFR (Instrument Flight Rules) pilots could land there. I called the First Baptist, talked to the pastor and soon a car came and took me to the church.

The pastor said, "We are having a special supper and mission study to night and would like for you to attend." In his introduction of me he said, "We have a missionary who just happened to dropped in on us tonight." Briefly, I told about my experiences and asked if I could give a testimony in song. My song was, "Precious Lord Take My Hand." It was a joyous night and a good meal also.

After the night in a local motel, I called Meacham Field again and got the same message as the day before. I called Ralph I told him my dilemma. "Take a bus home and I'll return for the plane later," he said. Getting on the bus, I bought a local newspaper and on the front page was a picture of a pilot killed the day before in the same weather I was in. I said a prayer for his family and hoped he didn't have any children. I thanked the Lord for my safety.

Several years later I came across Psalm 30 which is the perfect description of my experience. It says: "I will extol thee, O Lord, for thou **hast lifted me up,** and hast not made my foes to rejoice over me. O Lord my God, **I cried unto Thee** and thou hast healed me. O Lord, thou hast **brought up my soul from the grave; thou hast kept me alive, that I should not go down in the pit. Sing unto the Lord, O ye saints of his,** and give thanks at the remembrance of his holiness. For his anger endureth but a moment; **in his favor is life;** weeping may endure for a night, but **joy cometh in the morning.** And in my prosperity I said, I shall never be moved. Lord, by thy favor thou hast made my mountain to stand strong; **thou didst hide thy face and I was in trouble. I cried to thee O Lord; and unto the Lord I made my supplication. What profit is there in my blood when I go down to the pit? Shall the dust praise thee? Shall it declare thy truth?** Hear, O Lord and have mercy on me: Lord be thou my helper. **Thou hast turned for me my mourning into dancing: Thou hast put off my sackcloth and girded me with gladness;** to the end that my glory **may sing praise to thee, and not be silent,** O Lord my God, I will give thanks unto thee forever."

A week later I took the final flight examination, passed and received my license. I completed my studies at the seminary, and after visits with our families we returned to Colombia and the challenging work of teaching at the International Baptist Seminary in Cali, Colombia.

Quichua Revival

The city of Cali, surrounded by towering Andes mountains, is located in El Valle (The Valley) and is rich in orchards, sugar cane, and smooth Colombian coffee. Missionary Crea Ridenour describes Colombia, her adopted land:

"Land of the Condor, Beautiful land! Beautiful land!
Land of gold, land of abundance.
Land of blessings, illustrious,
Land that provided our sustenance."

I was initially called to the seminary to teach in the field of Religious Education but after a couple of years the seminary president, Dr. Ben Welmaker, asked me to teach his evangelism courses. Now my main responsibility became evangelism, for which I was glad. I was certified to teach Evangelism Explosion, an evangelism program developed by D. James Kennedy of Coral Ridge, Florida and the course was translated into Spanish and was a very useful evangelism tool for students and their churches. Frequent trips to a local prison gave students hands–on experience using evangelism lessons learned in class.

My most fruitful experience at the seminary began in the course called Methods of Church Growth. While discussing the chapter about Tent Evangelism I mentioned how exciting it would be to participate in a tent revival. A hand went up, and the student, David Fajardo, said, "A missionary in Ecuador named Jim Muse has a huge tent used for revivals with the Quichua Indians. He might let us use it."

I was excited at the prospect and called Jim in Quito. "Jim, this is Jim Oliver at the seminary in Cali. I'm teaching an evangelism class and David Fajardo is one of my students. He said you had a tent you use in revivals and maybe our class of five could come to Quito and work in one of your revivals. What do you say?"

"Great idea," said Jim. "I also have a camper that sleeps six making it less expensive for room and board."

At the end of the semester, four students and I loaded up the missionary van and left for Quito, Ecuador. The group consisted of David from Ecuador, Oscar Hall from San Andres Island, Jorge Laria from Colombia, Ainar Mina from Canada and me. Oscar played the guitar and we sang all the way to Quito.

Jim's camper was perfect, sleeping five comfortably and had a very adequate kitchen. We bought groceries like a family, prepared our meals, ate together, washed the dishes, made the beds, studied, prayed, preached and sang at the revival. I believe this is the closest I have been in preparing disciples as Jesus did. We hadn't finished our seminary text during the semester but were able to complete it that week.

Preaching and singing during the revival was outstanding and the tent was full every night and many Quichuas, men and women, made professions of faith. Each Quichua Church had two pastors and both were pleased at the results of the week and I was happy, along with the students.

Alcohol was a huge problem among the Indians. While visiting prospects in the little community of San Francisco de Conocoto we witnessed a Quichua "Religious" fiesta where the men were drunk and staggered around a field as the women sat watching. Sitting by one wife of a Quichua I asked if she believed God was pleased with the fiesta. I was surprised when she responded, "Yes, He's very pleased."

At the close of the Quichua revival I thanked Jim for all his help and encouragement and said, "We have a great need in Colombia for this type of ministry. Do you think it possible for us to borrow your tent for some campaigns?"

"I'll do better than that," he said. "Don Luis, a Colombian, is the man who puts the tent up and takes it down for me. I'll send him along to help you."

After our last service in Quito we traveled with the tent to a large Colombian city named Pasto. Missionaries Rick and Barbara McDade were very happy to have evangelistic tent revival in their city. The attendance was estimated at 1,300 with many making professions of faith. Our next stop was Popayan, the most Catholic city in Colombia. Attendance was around nine hundred but with fewer professions of faith. During the week our tent manager visited his home nearby, in the village of Piendamo, and won several family members to Christ. First Baptist Church in Cali heard about the new converts and sent Carlos Rozo, a member of the church, to establish a mission which became a thriving congregation. Returning to the seminary, the tent evangelists and I gave a report to students and faculty at a special chapel service.

Chapter

19

A Miracle

We missionaries were privileged to have good medical care in Colombia. Baptist physicians serving in the Clinic in Barranquilla were McGlamary, Kollmar, Breeden, Morris, Gustin, and Edwards. Nurses Arlene Rogers, Jennie Hester and Kay Brown also served in Barranquilla and Cartagena. One Colombian physician, Dr. Eduardo DeLima, lived a block from our home and made house calls when we needed a doctor. He and his American wife, Ellen, were not only professional blessings but friends.

One day I received a call from Dr. DeLima. "Ellen and I would like you and Marilyn to visit us tomorrow around 9 am. Think you can come?"

"Yes," I said. "See you at 9 o'clock."

To my surprise many friends from the seminary were present: Dr. Roy and Joyce Wyatt, Dr. Charles and Jean Allen, Dr. James and Mary Nell Giles, Dr. Ben and Janis Welmaker, and Dr. Allen and Virginia Neely. Upon arriving Dr. DeLima informed us his physician said he had a serious heart problem that required surgery in the United States.

"Our motive for asking you here," began the doctor, "is to ask you to pray for me."

Doctor DeLima knelt in the living room and we surrounded him, placing our hands on his head and shoulders and prayed silently. Then we held hands and sang a song of faith. Dr. DeLima had one more examination before he was to leave for the States and after those tests his physician said the trip should be postponed until more examinations were carried out. Soon it was discovered Dr. DeLima didn't need the operation and as far as I know he never made the trip. Dr. DeLima was cured.

Each year all Colombian missionaries met at the seminary in Cali to plan our budget and make personnel requests we felt necessary for our work. We always had a missionary speaker lead our devotionals and one year the New Testament professor, Dr. Hoke Smith led the study. I have been privileged to sit under the tutelage of many inspirational teachers in two seminaries but nothing touched me as deeply as Dr. Hoke Smith's exposition of the Book of Philippians. There were moments in his presentation I felt I was in the garden of Philippi, could see the oil lamps gently blowing in the breeze and was surrounded by my first–century brothers and sisters in Christ. Later his commentary was printed by The Baptist Publishing House in El Paso, Texas and today is an inspiration to many. Hoke died at a very young age leaving his wife, Wanda and four children. Wanda remained in Cali and taught music and Religious Education at the seminary for almost ten years after Hoke's death. She returned to the States when her son, Hoke Smith III was killed in a motorcycle accident.

One of my jobs at the seminary was Extension Director. I traveled to different cities for the purpose of setting up centers where pastors could study who were unable to attend the seminary in Cali. The most successful extension program was in Bogota, the capital, where Harry and Dona Harper taught classes in theology and Bob and Dolores McGee taught music. Another successful center was Barranquilla.

On one seminary extension trip to Bogota, I stayed in the home of missionaries Jimmy and Oneida Stiles. One night after dinner, Jimmy said a family he ministered to in the Colombian Plains would learn that night the prognosis of a very ill son. He asked if I would accompany him to see the boy. At the hospital we found sixty to seventy patients crowded together in a cold, cement building. After a long search we found Pepe, a six–year–old boy, that had been diagnosed with cancer. We stood by a cold, sick little boy with feeble arms raised crying for his father. Finally his father and doctor arrived and when asked about his son's condition, the doctor motioned for us to step aside. In a low voice, he told Pepe's father the cancer had spread through the boy's body and Pepe had only a few weeks to live. He then asked if he could make a suggestion. The father nodded. The doctor said, "We have done all possible for Pepe and I suggest your son be taken home to live out the remainder of his life around his family."

The doctor left and slowly we three walked out–side and under the bright stars and cold night of Bogota put our arms around a suffering father and cried. I saw Jimmy several months later and asked about Pepe. He said the father took the doctor's suggestion, took his son home where he died in his own bed surrounded by his mother, father, brothers and sisters. Pepe and his family were happy he had come home.

Chapter

20

Guajira Trip

Dan, Dave, John, and Jeannie, along with most of the missionary kids in Cali, attended a bilingual school named Bolivar. The classes were taught in English except for the Spanish class. The majority of the teachers were from the United States and usually had a two–year contract. Our children were blessed with exceptional, good teachers.

The choir teacher, Jana Shader, staged a major play each year using student actors. Roger Orr, Paul Magyar and our children participated in popular plays like *The Music Man, Godspell and Fiddler On The Roof.* The auditorium was always packed for the events.

A popular teacher was Phil Wielenga from Upper Peninsula, Michigan. Phil, a dedicated Christian, taught only one year at Bolivar but was so popular the yearbook was dedicated to him. Phil returned home and became a pilot with Delta Airlines. What a blessing he was and still is.

Bolivar initiated a field work program that was very educational. John Magyar and I were asked to lead a group of boys to the Guajira Peninsula with a side trip to Simon Bolivar's Museum in Santa Marta. Four missionary boys and two sons of Ron and Marlene Bundy made the trip. Dan's diary, in his own hand, tells the story.

My Diary From Cali To Guajira Peninsula

Danny Oliver

Introduction

This trip I am on covers about 1,300 miles of Colombia. I am taking it with 6 other boys. Their names are:

1. Roger Orr	4. Paul Magyar
2. Mark Bundy	5. John Magyar
3. Danny Allen	6. Tim Bundy

We also had 2 counselors with us

1. Jim Oliver	2. John Magyar

Our plans are to take a prop jet from Cali to Bogota. From Bogota to Santa Marta we will take a train and stay around there awhile. Then by car we will go up the Guajira and back to Barranquilla. From there we will come back by prop. The Guajira are said to be fierce at times. They like Ford Panel Trucks and we got one. They don't like friendliness and are true Nomads. They live in Colombia or Venezuela and have no license plates or papers like Cedulas and Passports. This diary is not to the very detail for I would think it impossible to explain most sights. Let's begin.

Sunday, June 25, 1973

That night we boarded the Aero Condor for Bogota. The pilot didn't know much because we fish tailed and hit pretty hard. Two families, Herndons and Harpers took us in. We split up in 2 groups and all of us slept for about the last time in a bed for a long time.

Monday 26, 1973

I woke up ready to go. We walked to visit the Gold Museum but it was closed so we went to Montserrat. That was great. The cable cars were something to ride on. This place has a church on top of the hill which is said is a place that can heal anything. We left and caught the train. Looks like we'll be up all night. This is why my writing is bad. This thing jerks everywhere. We had to guard our junk and try to sleep at the same time. It was beautiful and unexplainable.

Tuesday 27, 1973

I woke up at 5:30. I probably slept about 5 or 6 hours. This trip is great but its 22 hours long. We arrived in Santa Marta at 11:30. From 1:00 to 11:30 of jerking, sitting and eating not the greatest of meals we were all glad to crawl off that train. I still won't trade all the eggs in China. The man who was supposed to meet us was not there so we walked to the church. They gave us a class room for all of us to sleep in and we were happy after a good Pepsi.
We all decided to go to "Rodadero." That's the area outside of town where everybody swims. We went to catch the bus at the train station while one of our counselors bought a bathing suit. After 40 minutes of waiting we saw Jim Harless pull up. He was to pick us up. We all got in and when Uncle John came back with his suit we went to Rodadero. We swam and built sand castles and had a blast. Then without Mr. Harless we went to eat at "Los Cumbieros." It was terrible service and broke the maximum amount of money to be spent for eating. $30.

Was the maximum. We spent $50. We went back to the church after a short ride. I slept on a hard floor.

Wednesday 28, 1973

I woke up at 6:30. I was one of the first so I worked on the Sterno Stove and was one of the first 3 to get breakfast. After about ten pieces of bacon we all packed. I worked on my diary and got it up to date. Then I packed and got in the car with all the others and we headed for the Guajiros as we had planned. We had heard these people were really nomads and hated to be friendly. The drive was really neat. We stopped at many towns. After Riohacha we started seeing many Guajiros. Some men wore plain clothes and others wore just a tiny little loin cloth. We asked 2 if we could take their pictures but the lady ran away and the man acted like he didn't understand us. The counselors threw out a lot of tracts to street walkers. The land here is perfect desert.

I've never seen a better desert than this one. We took a few pictures on the way and saw many Indian chaps. The next big city was Maicao. We stopped at a nice store. It had a lot of American products. The people got them from Venezuela. Venezuela was 11 miles from there but some guys did not have any papers with them so we didn't go. We took a side road to Uribia but on the way found a good camping site so we stayed there. After supper when all tents were up we were put on watches. We all took turns and boy we were scared. Think if you are about 100 yards from camp looking with your flashlight for some Guajitos. After my watch I slept. That was from 2 to 4:30.

Thursday 29, 1973

After a 4:30 breakfast we finished the drive to Uribia. All roads from here were dirt. This town did not have many Guajiros. The next town was Manaure. It is their headquarters. This is where the salt harvest is. The people there were strange. We came to where they harvesting salt and what a cite. I can't explain much in this diary but for one thing this was a great adventure. We took a road where all the salt was piled by it and also Guajiros. They weren't doing anything but staring back coldly. Then Counselor John handed them a track and before long all of them were reaching for tracks and grabbing and everything. After about 75 yards the trail ended. We thought we were in a fix but we backed out of it in reverse. They were grabbing tracks from all of us now. They could have robbed our watches but they did not get anything. We had made friends. We drove around taking pictures of people, talking to them and handing out tracks. A man who we gave tracks to gave us a lot of salt. After that we left for Riohacha then Santa Marta. After getting groceries we left for Villa Concha. There we set up camp and swam 15 feet from the shore and the water over your head. Fish are everywhere around. We ate a great meal and then caught crabs and blew them up with firecrackers. My watch was 2 to 3 o'clock but I wasn't scared any. After that I fell asleep till about 7:00.

Friday 30, 1973

I was waken up next morning by my Dad. He was wearing goggles and had just taken a swim and observing the fish. Allen woke up and we both went out. It was really cool. After breakfast and a shower we all decided to go to Santa Marta and look for some goggles and some hot dogs. We looked all around Santa Marta and decided to go back after buying groceries. Oh, I almost forgot the Simon Bolivar Museum. We went there and got a guide for $15 or something like that. He told us everything and it was real historical. We saw where he ate, slept and fooled around his last 11 days. We made friends with our guide and he showed us million of things we would have missed. After that we went back and ate hot dogs. After a lot of swimming all us guys went down the beach and to a little lagoon. What we spotted amazed us. There were about 10 million crabs with pinchers as big as your hands. We caught 8 of them. We climbed the rocks for about 20 minutes and after all that time we found a good rock to dive off of. It had 3 levels. We took turns diving and then went back. We put the 8 crabs in a castle to watch them fight. They didn't and all of them probably got out 1 hour after we left. We sat on the pier and talked and then went to take watches and sleep. We had heard the other night a camp got all its stuff stolen so we were wide awake. Our friends slept there all night and their stuff got stolen from under them.

All night they came walking in and asking for something. Some for gas, some for a piece of wood from the fire and some for the kicks. They were all looking for some of our stuff. We had them fooled. Two kids came in during Johnny's and my watch but we got rid of them. Otherwise, the night was uneventful because I snuck in a tent and slept.

Saturday July 1, 1973

I was up at 7:00 and after scrambled eggs and strawberry juice we all went out and took our last swim. That didn't last but about 90 minutes and since I was almost completely packed up I took a great warm bath. After it I rolled up my sleeping bag and stuck in my 2 pair of dry shoes and bathing suit and towel in my pack and then packed them in the car. We left for Barranquilla. We got to Santa Marta and ate hamburgers and then we were on a two hour drive to my first hometown. I had lived there for 4 years of my life and loved it. On this highway each side had a great body of water. Lake Cienaga and the Caribbean Sea were on opposite sides. We waited for the ferry about 10 minutes till we could cross over the Magdalena River. The 1 mile bridge was almost finished there. We got to the Wares house and got in our normal groups. Roger, Mark, Counselor Jim and me stayed at the Wares and the rest at the Harless. After fixing our beds our group went and met at the Harless. We ate some great hamburgers and then all 9 of us came together and told of our great adventurous trip. After all this it was about 10:00 and so we went back to the Wares and slept good. At least I did.

SUNDAY 2, 1973

I was awaken by the sound of voices and found I was right by the breakfast table. I went up stairs, took a bath and came back and ate with

Roger and Mark. I ate 2 eggs, Frosted Flakes, and for the 2 time coffee for breakfast. Man that junks gross as heck. After breakfast the other group came over for church at home. Mr. Harless gave his testimony of how he turned to Jesus as Savior and it was interesting and short. After church we all went or stayed in our homes to pack for leaving while the counselors went to a second church. It seemed about 10 minutes before they came back but all of us were ready so we left for a Chinese Rest. to eat. We found one and I stuffed myself up till I could pop. I waddled out to the car, could barely fit in the doorway. We left for the airport. At the airport was a man who smoked a cig a minute but he was an American and very interesting. On our plane a Catholic Choir of 50 girls got on. Not one of us sat by each other. Those girls were really good and we had a fun time talking and all that. I saw one barf right in the aisle but it was probably her first flight. After landing between a wall of mountains in Medellin and right on one in Pereira we were on the last leg homeward.

It rained hard on the way to Cali and puddles were everywhere there. Even though some families were flooded out they came and met us there. My dad (Jim the Counselor) had got another plane to stay in Medellin for a day so

I had to tell the trip to mom and brothers and sister. What a beautiful trip. I had just tons of experiences but there was no place like home.

THE END

Epilogue

This trip is over and I am at home now living it up. All through this trip something was happening to learn of.

There is a lot to learn on trips like this and no one alive could tell you everything that happened. You would have to be with me and then not even your mind will remember it all. This diary is the last thing from full detail but I hope you enjoyed reading it.

Danny Oliver

Chapter

21

Sad Story

I WISH I COULD say all missionaries exemplify holiness and godliness throughout their lives but unfortunately it isn't true. When a missionary falls it's not the rule but thank the Lord, an exception. This is the story of a fallen missionary.

I'll call him "Shamma," which in Hebrew means, desolation. I got to know Shamma as we made several trips together to the coastal city of Buenaventura where I helped him clear his family goods through customs. After Shamma, wife, and son had lived in Cali a few years, we received news they were separating. The word was Shamma was sending his wife and son home and remaining in Cali with another woman. We were greatly sadden. We prayed and much counsel was offered but nothing changed.

One night I told Marilyn I would visit Shamma and try to get through to him even if it took all night. I arrived at 9 p.m., after their son was in bed. We sat in the kitchen and talked for a long time and around midnight I thought I saw a ray of hope. I said, "It's seems we are getting somewhere and the solution to the problem is near."

Arrogantly Shamma blurted out, "Nothing has changed. My wife and son are returning home and I'm staying here."

The Bible says, "Be angry..." and now I was very angry. A famous preacher once said, "Worldly anger is set on the fire of hell; holy anger borrows flame from the alter fires of God." I prayed the latter was true for my anger.

However, the remainder of the verse says, "but sin not," and here was where I failed, and failed miserably. The thought invading my mind was I wanted to take this guy outside and punish him with some lessons I had learned in the Army. He was younger and I knew he would probably cleanup the street up with me but I decided it would be worth it if I could just get in one good blow. It got worse.

Trying to entice him outside I called him a bad word. Shamma's wife bowed her head and silently cried but Shamma didn't move. We sat silently for what seemed like an eternity. Satan won a victory that night in the lives of two people, Shamma and me.

The next morning I arrived early at the seminary for my class and was surprised to meet a fellow colleague at the door. "Jim, guess who just came by to see me?" Before I could answer, he said, "Shamma was here and told me what you called him last night." He leaned closer and whispered, "You should have called him something worse." I didn't feel any better.

More about this family came out later. Shamma's wife returned to the states with her son, completed a college degree and got a job teaching school. She remarried and all were happy for her and her son. Later, an amazing story about Shamma came to light. The missionary that took my evangelism class also took students to preach at the prison told me later they found Shamma in jail. He had broken a law and in Colombia you are guilty until proven innocent. I never heard the end of the story. I'm reminded of the verse, "Whatsoever a man sows, that shall he also reap." I pray Shamma will repent, asking God's forgiveness for abandoning his wife and son. I prayed earnestly the Lord would also forgive me.

Chapter

22

Amazon Trip

Son Dan had a question. "Dad, do you know how close we are to the greatest river in the world, the Amazon?" Dan was a junior in Bolivar High School in Cali and was scheduled to return with us on our next furlough and graduate a year later in Montgomery. He would then enter college at Auburn in Alabama after we returned to Cali.

"No, how close are we?" I asked.

Holding up two fingers about two inches apart he said, "This close."

Checking the map, I found Cali was really that close to the Great River. "You are right. What does that mean?"

"It would be sad, if living so close, we never saw it."

Here was a challenge. Would it be possible to take some boys to the Amazon River? Who would go and what would it cost? Alone in the cool of the night, I studied the map to find not only the most economical but also the most exciting and educational route. My plan was to travel by bus from Cali to the Colombian border town of Ipiales, cross over to Tulcan, Ecuador and spend the first night in Quito. From Quito we would continue by bus to our second stop-over, Guayaquil, Ecuador, and then continue South to Chiclayo, Peru. From Chiclayo we would fly to Iquitos, Peru, a city on the Amazon River. In Iquitos we would take a four–day boat trip down river to Leticia, Colombia and after a few days rest and exploration of the town and river we would fly back to Bogota and then home. I estimated we could make the trip in two weeks.

I checked the cities where we planned to make overnight stops and found names and addresses of missionaries I believed might take poor wandering nomads in and perhaps provide a meal and a place to lay their tired heads. I wrote to them about our dream and was greatly encouraged by their response. They all said, "Come on down. We have a place for you."

I asked the boys who should we invite to make the trip with us? Besides our three, there were six other boys in the Cali missionary family that I was sure would love to go. Ten would make a good, round number. After explaining my plans to Dan, Dave and John, they excitedly spread the news to all their buddies. Returning from their missionary efforts to enlist their friends, I was discouraged to learn none of the six missionary kids got permission from their parents to strike out with us. We decided this would not stop us. The last day of school we received news that two of Dan's class mates were interested in the trip. Kirk Schlup and Tony Docal's fathers, both tire manufacturing executives, agreed their sons could make the trip. Excited, we now had a team; Kirk, Tony, Dan, Dave, John and me.

At a meeting with the parents I presented the planned route and the estimated cost of the trip; two hundred dollars a person. This included food, bus tickets, lodging when necessary and four air fares. The trip would begin on the evening of June 18, 1975 and the estimated return was July 1. We needed to travel light, taking only the bare necessities which included a personal sleeping bag for each traveler. The day before we were to leave, Dan fainted at a camp, splitting his chin, requiring twelve stitches to close. Dr. Farabella of Cali, gave him penicillin pills to take every hour and sent him to bed. We wondered if Dan could make the trip but when he awoke the next morning he felt better and the doctor gave permission for him to go.

On June 18, all the travelers and their families met at the bus station in Cali at 5:40 p.m. for our departure. Joyce Wyatt and James Giles also wished us Bon Voyage and treated us to a box of baked chicken and Cokes. We were off on time, sitting directly behind the bus driver. The trip would take all night and no one slept because the driver's radio blared from the beginning of the trip to the end. No one complained because the radio not only kept us awake all night but also our driver. Around midnight we took rest stops in the sleepy towns of Popayan and Pasto.

At 8 am we arrived at the border town of Ipiales, Colombia and walked in a cold, drizzling rain to DAS, the Colombian Police station where we presented our papers to cross the Ecuador. The officer in charge informed us we didn't have the correct papers and we had to return to Cali for them. Shocked, we stood around wondering what to do next. If we returned to Cali it would be the end of our trip. Finally, the officer in charge left and I approached the second in command and asked again if we could continue our trip. He informed me if he let us go and was caught, it would cost him a day's wages. This he repeated several times until I finally got the message. "How much is a day's wages?" I asked.

"Ten thousand pesos (about eight dollars)," he said.

I said, "If we paid the day's wages would you let us go?"

Happily he said, "Yes." We paid the day's wages, he stamped our papers and the entrance into Ecuador at Tulcan went smoothly.

Several told us the best bus to Quito was the Expreso so we bought the tickets and boarded. Those who said the Expreso was the best didn't mean the fastest but the one that stopped at every village and town from Tulcan to Quito. Instead of arriving at Quito in three hours it took us eight. We did get an education about small towns in Ecuador that few have experienced – or want to experience.

Richard and Barbara Clements, our Big Brother and Sister in Language School, greeted us with a nourishing meal and comfortable beds. After a good night's sleep and a breakfast of hot pancakes and sausage, Barbara took us on a tour of Quito. First we visited the Metropolitan Cathedral constructed in baroque style in the seventeenth century. The ashes of the Great Marshall of Ayacucho, Jose de Sucre and General Juan Jose Flores, the first president of Ecuador were buried there.

Next we visited the middle of the earth, the Equator. Over the dry landscape at 0" 0' 0" stands a memorial to the labor of the scientists from the French Academy who determined the "middle of the earth." Each of us had our picture taken with one foot in the Northern hemisphere and the other in the Southern. Our visit in Quito with the Clements was over too soon and on June 22 we boarded a bus going South towards the city of Guayaquil, Ecuador, home of Stanley and Glenna Stamps.

Our second bus trip in Ecuador was the most comfortable. We were treated with breathtaking scenery as we passed one banana plantation after another surrounded by the high Andes Mountains. I had been told Ecuador was one of the biggest banana exporting countries in the world and after that trip I believe it. Arriving in Guayaquil we were met by Stanley and taken to his home where we met his wife Glenna and their children Keith, Mark and Rhonda Lynn. The next day, Sunday, I was asked to preach at Urdesa Baptist Church in Guayaquil. Stanley loaned me a coat to wear for the service and if I remember correctly, it was a little large for me. After lunch we were given a tour of Guayaquil, taking pictures of the statues of the two liberators of South America, Simon Bolivar and San Martin. The statues commemorate the one and only meeting of the two famous liberators. We didn't have time to fish in the nearby Gulf of Guayaquil where record–size marlins are caught almost daily. Since that day I have planned to return to this fisherman's paradise but haven't made it yet.

Early Monday morning, the 24 of June, we ate a delicious breakfast prepared by Glenna and were taken to the bus station by Stanley. Our next stop was Chiclayo, Peru, home of Jim and Linda Boswell. This wasn't the best planned part of the trip since we arrived in Chiclayo at 4 a.m. and didn't have Boswell's address. I finally got a call through to missionary Irvin Northcutt in Trujillo who gave us the address and phone number of the Boswells. Later we arrived at the home of the Boswell's to find them away on vacation. They were expecting us and had left a note saying we would be well taken care of by Lilly Bran, a summer missionary from Aims, Iowa. Lilly was a real angel of mercy who took us on a tour of the city and we treated her to dinner that evening.

The Boswells returned early from their vacation because of sickness but before we left they encouraged us to make the trip to the nearby city of Cajamarca, home of the Inca King Atahualpa. We made the trip and were glad we did. We sat on Atahualpa's throne and visited the room where he raised his hand signifying the height his people would fill the room with gold, silver and precious stones if the Spanish Conquistadores freed him. The red mark around the room where the king raised his hand is still there. The Spaniards agreed to the pact and the room was filled with riches but the Spaniards reneged on their part and strangled King Atahualpa. A very dark day in Spanish history.

During our visit in Cajamarca, a young boy named Edison was our unofficial guide. We told him we had very little money for a tip but he still insisted on showing us all the interesting sights. We learned a lot from Edison and were able to provide a decent tip. When it was time to leave for Trujillo we discovered the taxi we contracted had already gone and the only taxi left was much more expensive. Quickly we ran to the bus station and bought the last six tickets for Trujillo. Lazily walking around town, I told the boys we had money for food or a motel room but not both and asked which they preferred. Naturally they all opted for food. After eating we were looking for a church to sleep in when we ran into Edison who was surprised to see us. After telling him our story he said his grandparents might let us stay in their house for the night and thankfully, in an unfinished room, we bedded down in our sleeping bags.

The next morning, at the break of dawn, we ran to the station and boarded the bus. As we waited about forty indigenous Indians came into town singing and stopped at our bus. The natural harmony of their voices, accompanied by their flutes and guitars touched the depth of our hearts as the rising sun saluted us announcing a new day. A spiritual peace and joy flooded our souls.

The trip from Cajamarca to Trujillo was one long, hot journey through more desert any of us had seen or could image. In Trujillo we were met by Irvin and Mildred Northcutt who put us up in comfortable rooms at the theological school he directed. The next morning we were surprised by a breakfast that would top them all. Irvin began the breakfast by preparing a huge plate of bacon followed by a mountain of scrambled eggs. Then came three plates of hot toast with homemade strawberry jam. To that was added coffee, milk and bowls of cream of wheat. Irvin's breakfast won the prize for the best meal of the trip.

On June 28, my forty–third birthday, Irvin took us to the seven–hundred–year–old ruins of the Pre–Inca Chimu Indians. After our refreshing and memorable visit with the Northcutts we boarded a DC–3 airplane that took us to a little town of Tarapoto, Peru. This was a necessary trip since we couldn't get a direct flight to Iquitos. Each of us breathed through an oxygen tube as our plane passed over the 14,800 foot Peruvian Mt. Payne. Our next stop, after leaving Tarapoto, was in the small town of Juanjui where the boys agreed would be the perfect place for their honeymoon. The only exciting event in Juanjui was the once a week landing of the DC-3 for which all the town turned out to see. We rented a cheap motel where we washed our clothes, which had become a dire necessity. Two days later we boarded a smaller plane that took us to our destination, Iquitos, Peru and the mighty Amazon.

In Iquitos I had arranged for us to stay in the guest house owned and operated by the Independent Baptist Mission of Peru, Miss Ellen Morgan, hostess. Kurt, Tony, Dan and Dave had the largest bedroom and John and I shared the smaller one. After settling in, we walked to the Amazon and got our first sight of the river–sea. A few miles from Iquitos the river makes a sharp right turn and flows toward the Atlantic Ocean, two thousand miles away. The Amazon begins from a few melted ice drops on the Mismi Mountain high in the Peruvian Andes and is fed by 1,001 tributaries as it traverses through Peru, Colombia and Brazil. When it reaches the Atlantic Ocean it pushes fresh water over a hundred miles out to sea. The Amazon has one–fifth of all the river water in the world and this is what we planned to travel on.

At the guest house we had kitchen privileges which cut down on food expenses and turned us into short–order cooks as well as dishwashers. We learned the market prices and how to bargain with the natives. The first evening meal consisted of soup, crackers and cheese sandwiches and since it had been a hard day we retired early. It was difficult to get the boys up for breakfast until I hit upon the solution. "The last one in the kitchen has to wash dishes," was motivation enough for the week. Two were appointed to go to the market with me where we bought fresh oranges, bananas and coffee, but found no sugar. We also bought fresh eggs, bread, homemade jam, crackers and more soup. We drew straws to see who would prepare the meals.

After breakfast we began the search for the boat to take us to Leticia, Colombia. We weren't prepared for the news that the Peruvian government had banned all boats leaving Iquitos for all destinations downriver. We heard later this temporary law had been declared because animals and exotic birds were being smuggled out of the country. We were very discouraged but all we could do was wait and see if the law would change. The next three days went by slowly with a little sightseeing in Iquitos which isn't known as a tourist paradise. The town was overrun with motorized rickshaws carrying people everywhere, most doing business related to the Amazon. A couple of five–story office buildings were built on the Amazon River.

Chinese restaurants were everywhere and we soon found one we liked. Since money was running low, we ordered Wonton Fritos and ate so many we all agreed never to eat Wonton Fritos again. That was good for us because we began to eat more like the natives: bananas, mangos, papaya, rice and black beans. Each day after breakfast we walked to the river only to hear the travel law was still in force, no boat was going East on the river. On the forth day something very interesting happened.

While resting in our room we had a visitor, Amazon missionary Duane Ruder. He informed us he had a boat but it was out of service for a month. He told us about an idea that would get us to Leticia. We could buy a balsa wood raft for twenty dollars and float down the river arriving at our designation in a matter of days. He said, "There's only one problem: ships coming upriver at night could run over you but that could be remedied by hanging lanterns on a pole. They would see you and go around."

He also said, "The Amazon flows one and one-half miles an hour making the trip no longer than eight days and nights." We were so excited we could hardly sleep. Kirk said this was a story he would tell his grandchildren one day.

Early the next day we made a list of what would be needed for the trip: two machetes, rope (two meters), a small grill, frying pan, water (2 ½ gallons), two flashlights, fishing line and hooks, two gallons of kerosene, matches, hard soap, toilet paper, plastic bags, six glasses, forks, plates, suntan lotion and a can opener.

After breakfast we went looking for the raft and were told a salesman by the river would sell us one. We entered a small office overlooking the Amazon and met a jolly gentleman sitting behind a desk smoking a cigar.

In broken English he said, "What can I do for you gentlemen?"

'We're looking for a balsa wood raft," I said. "I understand you can buy one for twenty dollars."

"That's true, "he said. "What do you plan to do with the raft?"

"We plan to make a trip on it from here to Leticia, Colombia."

"Is this your first time on the Amazon?" he asked.

"Yes," I answered.

"Do you plan to hire a guide?"

"No sir. We don't have enough money for a guide."

With a big smile on his face he said, "Don't worry. I have been in this business for many years and have always been able to find rafts for my customers. Come back early in the morning."

Wasting no time the nest day we rushed early to the salesman's office. There we were greeted with a sad face. "Gentlemen," he began. "This is the most unusual thing I have ever seen in my life. I have looked far and wide for your raft and I must tell you there is not one raft for sale in a hundred mile radius of this city. I'm really sorry you can't make the trip." We returned to the Chinese restaurant and ate some more Wonton Fritos.

The only option left was to take a plane to Leticia. I bought the tickets early the next morning, paid Miss Morgan for our room and hired a couple of rickshaws to take us to the airport. The short flight to Leticia was a fascinating experience as we passed low over mile after mile of the meandering and awe-inspiring Amazon River.

I was told an American named Mike Tsalickis lived in Leticia and legally trapped and exported reptiles, animals and birds to zoos in the United States. Mike is a legend, thanks to pictures and articles in National Geographic and Life Magazine. He owned a motel and a restaurant in Leticia as well as directing guided tours on the Amazon River and the jungle. It was rumored he gave missionaries 25% discount on room, board and tours. Upon our arrival in Leticia I was surprised when a man approached me and asked, "Are you a missionary?"

I said, "Yes."

He said, "I'm from Mike's motel."

I said, "Let's go."

At the motel we were told a tour of the Amazon was ready to leave and asked if we wanted to go. We threw our bags in the room, paid the fee and took off. The tour lasted four hours and what we saw and experienced can never be explained by mere words. A light lunch and drink was served as we crisscrossed the mighty river. We entered mysterious tributaries, passed Monkey Island, the natural breeding ground of the squirrel monkey, and saw a seaplane take off in the middle of the river. We met Englishmen casting hand nets to catch tropical fish to take back to their aquariums. They looked a little anxious each time they drew the net in wondering if it was full of piranhas or an angry electric eel.

Back at the motel we relaxed around Mike's swimming pool surrounded by a wide thatch canopy with tree slab tables. We took pictures of macaw sitting on our shoulders hoping they wouldn't take a bite out of an ear. Sitting by Mike at supper I said, "What's the possibility of a raft trip from Iquitos to Leticia?"

"It is possible but two things are necessary for the trip. First, you must stop at night and mark on your river map your location. Second, an outboard motor is necessary to get you back in the main current of the river when you drift into slow eddies." Ever since that time I have been looking for volunteers to raft down the Amazon, but so far have had only a few takers.

We enjoyed the visit with Mike and company but soon it was time to say goodbye and return home. Before leaving, I bought a snake skin, a blow gun and a bark painting from Mike's jungle shop. On the trip back to Bogota we flew over the vast Amazon jungle, a spectacular sight that stretched mile after mile after mile. I pray there will be an Amazon jungle for years to come, enjoyed by those who live and visit there.

In Bogota we boarded the plane to Cali, our last leg of the trip. When we arrived we were met by Kirk and Tony's parents along with Marilyn and Jeannie. It was July 7, 1975; twenty days after our departure. Twenty days of thrills, enjoyment, danger; twenty days five guys and one guide will never forget.

Chapter

23

MOTHER'S MIDNIGHT RIDE

ONE YEAR, BAPTISTS in South America sponsored a Religious Education Conference in Buenos Aires, Argentina and I was selected to represent our seminary. Upon hearing this, Marilyn said, "I believe you need someone to help with the luggage," or something like that. The conference began in January 1974 but we had a problem; who would take care of the children while we were away. Mother and Dad to the rescue. After a quick call they began packing for their Cali adventure.

The day they were to arrive, excitement mounted as we piled into the missionary van to make the forty minute drive to the airport. At the airport we rushed to the waiting area overlooking the runway to get the best view. We watched with great anticipation as the Avianca plane from Bogota touched down. I said to the kids, "I believe the next passengers to get off will be your grandparents." That relieved some anxiety but when the last passenger deplaned and still no sight of grandparents, we began to worry. Could we be mistaken about the date, time or flight number? I told Marilyn to wait in the car with the children while I checked the passenger list.

As I waited at the Avianca desk a woman approached me and asked if I was Mr. Oliver? I said yes and she began telling me the story. "I was on the plane with your parents and after landing in Bogota, your mother asked me to get off and accompany her to get a coke. In the crowded airport we were separated so I returned to the plane. Your dad asked me to return and have her paged, which I did but with no success. Upon returning to the plane the flight attendant told your dad he had to get off and look for his wife because the plane had to go on to Cali. Your dad got off the plane and that was the last time I saw him."

By the time I got to the car I was in shock. Mother and dad were somewhere in Bogota but in what condition? The city of Bogota has twice the population of the state of Alabama and the dangers of this South American capital cannot be over–emphasized, especially for supposedly "rich foreigners" who don't speak the language. Like all cities that size there are daily robberies, kidnappings and murders. It was midnight before we returned home but immediately I called Jimmy Stiles in Bogota. Jimmy grew up near the

Mexican border and could speak better Spanish than many Colombians. He had an adventurous spirit and if anyone could find mom and dad, it was Jimmy.

"Jimmy, this is Jim Oliver in Cali. I hate to bother you this late but I have a problem. My mother and dad got off the plane in Bogota and we haven't heard from them. Think you could find them?"

"Do my best, Jim."

Believing everything was under control, Marilyn and I went to bed. About 2 a.m. the phone rang and it was Jimmy. "Found your Dad and he's here with me. He wants to talk to you."

"Jimmy, this is your Dad. Is your mother there?"

"No Dad, but what you must do is get the first flight to Cali in the morning and if she isn't here by then I'll return to Bogota and look for her."

Now there would be no more sleeping. Around 3 a.m. Marilyn and I lay staring at the ceiling wondering what would happen next when we heard a car drive up. Someone got out and we heard, "Put my bags on the front porch and thank ya'll for bringing me home. Have a good night." It was mother. After a very warm welcome we called dad saying mom had arrived safely.

"Tell her, I want a word with her when I get there," he said.

As tired as we were, we had to hear mom's story. She began. "After being separated in the airport from my friend, I followed some passengers and found a seat on a plane. I sat down and when asked where I was going, I said Cali. I was told the plane wasn't going to Cali but I still didn't get off. The plane stopped three times and when it landed in Cali I saw all my luggage. Two men and one woman from the airlines were with me and when I showed them the directions to your house, they brought me here."

The next morning I met a tired dad getting off the plane with three Colombians following, arms loaded with all his carry–on packages. He was so glad to see mother he forgot his sermon.

His story was as amazing as mother's. He said, "When I got off the plane in Bogota´ I had no idea what to do next. As I looked around at all the people, a stranger walked up and in English asked if I needed help. Hearing my story he took me to the Avianca desk and when they heard about my plight told the stranger to take me to a hotel in town. I hadn't been there long before Jimmy came by and picked me up. I was glad to see him and talk to you later."

During the two weeks we were away, mom and dad took good care of their four grandchildren. After the children were safely off to school, mother would go down to the corner, catch the first bus that came by and ride around town looking at all the sights. When she tired, she hailed a taxi, showed him directions to the house, give him ten dollars and said, "Thank you for bringing me home."

When I heard about mother's trips, I asked, "Mother, what if the bus you got on wasn't a city bus but one going sixty miles away to Popayan. What would you have done?"

"I would tell them I live in Cali. Please take me home."

Mom and dad's visit was a blessings to us and especially for our children who got to know them better. That summer dad and mom attended a Gideon's Retreat in Shocco Springs, the Baptist Assembly in Alabama, where mother played the piano. During that retreat, mother suffered a massive heart attack and died. When I got the news, I rushed home for the funeral but couldn't believe she was gone until I entered the church. Someone was playing the organ but the piano bench was vacant. I've often wondered if God had to assign more angels to watch over mother in heaven than she had on earth.

Chapter 24

Colombian Violence

THE DRUG WAR intensified after our first ten years in Colombia. In Cali one morning, we were all going about our business as usual. The kids were in school, I was in my office at the seminary and Marilyn was home. All of a sudden we heard a noise from the street that sounded like gun shots.

Causally we went outside and found a car crashed into a tree. Looking inside we found a dead woman slumped over the steering wheel and a small boy crying by her side. Neighbors quickly took the boy to their home and called the police. The newspaper reported the murdered woman was the wife of a criminal drug dealer that had left the country pursued by other insurgents. Unable to punish their enemy, they took revenge on his wife. As far as we know the murderers were never caught.

Wycliffe missionaries have been active in Colombia for years translating the scriptures for many indigenous tribes. They have experienced opposition by many Colombian citizens as well as government leaders. Wycliffe missionaries Chester Bitterman and wife were translating the scripture from their mission base in Loma Linda but needed more supplies and a well deserved rest.

In Bogota they resided in the Guest Apartments while they shopped. One day a couple of men appeared at the apartment looking for the director of Wycliffe. Chester met them at the door and informed them the director wasn't there. The men immediately took Chester leaving behind his wife and children. Negotiations went on for several weeks with threats to kill Chester if all the Wycliffe missionaries didn't leave Colombia. When the demands were not met they took Chester out one Sunday morning, put him on a bus and shot him in the heart.

The response of Chester's family made national news. Though deeply sadden they showed no bitterness and later donated a special bus to the city of Bogota in memory of their son. Years later, while serving in Cartagena, we worked with a volunteer mission group that wanted to work in Colombia because Chester was a graduate of the university where they attended.

A few years after the death of Chester, one in our Colombia family was a victim of the enemy of Christ's servants. Missionary Charley Hood had served several years as Bookstore manager in Bogota but was preparing for a new job in evangelism and church planting. One morning he heard a strange noise in the front yard and stepping out side saw two men on a motorcycle. One pulled out a pistol and fired one shot, hitting Charley in the heart. Charley left a wife, two children and an unfinished job.

A dedicated layman of Cartagena, Luis Diaz, told us the story of a brother that was kidnapped and held for ransom. The insurgents demands were unmet and were ready to kill his brother when the Colombian police arrived. The kidnappers were all killed but not before killing Luis' brother. The policemen found his body had been tied to the ground several days not allowing him to relieve himself.

The reaction of many Colombian families experiencing such crimes was search out the kidnappers and execute them on the spot. Luis' reaction was just the opposite. He, and his wife Aide, began a church in their home and today it is thriving and seeing lives changed through the grace of Jesus Christ.

Marilyn and I had one possible encounter with the rebels. It was very dangerous traveling the highways outside the cities the last four years we were in Colombia. Many cars and buses were stopped, robbed and sometimes burned. Some passages were kidnapped and a few killed. On one emergency trip, Marilyn and I were returning to Cartagena on a country road when we came upon a road block surrounded either by Colombia soldiers or rebels. A man with a rifle approached us and asked, "Do you have a weapon?"

I said, "No."

He then asked, "What do you have in the trunk?"

"Why don't we look," I said.

I opened the trunk and showed him Bibles and Christian magazines. "Look," I said. "We want you and your men to take all this material you want." Several took Bibles and others magazines.

He then asked, "How long have you been in Colombia?"

"Almost thirty years," I said.

He laughed and said, "You're more Colombia than me. I'm not thirty years old." Turning to his men he said, "What you say we let'em go?" They nodded in agreement. Leaving in somewhat of a hurry, we turned to see them looking over their new gifts.

Chapter
25

The Archipelago Adventure

After much prayer and soul–searching, I felt the Lord calling me back to my first love, starting churches and helping them grow. I thoroughly enjoyed the ten years I served as professor at the seminary and knew there was a need preparing men and women for the ministry but I had to return to what I believed God wanted me to do. It was hard leaving my work and fellowship with the seminary professors and students. As usual, Marilyn agreed with my conviction and together we said goodbye to our beloved seminary colleagues and students.

After prayer and a long discussion with our area director, Bryan Brasington, we were assigned to the Colombian

Archipelago, San Andres, Providence and Santa Catalina Islands. At that time there were nine strong English speaking Baptist churches on San Andres and only one Spanish church. Our main job was to start another Spanish church on the island and help the English churches with evangelism and Sunday School outreach. San Andres is an island nine miles long and three miles wide and at that time had a population of seventy thousand, one half English-speaking islanders and the other half Spanish speakers from the Colombian mainland.

San Andres Island first appeared on maps in 1527 and is located one hundred miles east of Nicaragua and three hundred miles north of the Colombian mainland. Providence and its sister island, Santa Catalina, are located forty miles north of San Andres. San Andres, a tourist attraction, was declared a Free Port in 1953, making it even more popular.

Puritan colonists settled in Providence Island in 1627 and later in San Andres. Scottish descendant Philip Beekman Livingston, Jr. was destined to change the lives of countless thousands on the Colombian Islands. As a seaman, Phillip, Jr. sailed to New York and was converted and baptized in a Baptist church. Returning home to San Andres, Phillip became minister, teacher and doctor of the islands. A historic church building, the First Baptist of San Andres, was built in Mobile, Alabama, dismantled and shipped to San Andres. Church members pulled the building, piece–by–piece up to the highest point of the island, reassembled it and now the church stands as a lighthouse for the gospel of Jesus Christ to all islanders and tourists.

One of the strongest Baptist churches in the Colombian Convention is the English speaking First Baptist Church of San Andres and many outstanding pastors have come from there and other churches of the islands. Marilyn and I felt led to become members at the First Baptist though we spent most of our time ministering to the new Spanish church where we were called. The Spanish church grew fast and a local islander, Ricardo Gordon, seminary graduate, became its first pastor soon after the work began.

Our third year on San Andres, our pastor, Cipriano Stevens, felt led to take a course of Religious Education at New Orleans Baptist Seminary and the church called me as interim pastor. Later Cipriano returned to complete his degree in New Orleans and I was called upon again. Being pastor of that great historical church was a challenge and unique blessing.

The pastor of the First Spanish Church of San Andres was Oscar Hall, my student at the seminary and one of the five that made the trip to Quito for the tent revival. One day I said, "Oscar, let's pray about the evangelism ministry of the islanders and see if there is an interest among the pastors to see if they would adopt the Evangelism Explosion program in their churches." All the pastors enthusiastically approved the plan and we began training them and their members. I have never witnessed a more successful combined effort of evangelism in my ministry. During the study an important project was all trainees had to go out in teams of three each night, share the gospel to someone and seek a decision for Christ. After about two hours of visitation the teams returned and gave their reports to all those taking the course. Many nights we didn't finish our victorious testimonies until midnight but I never heard one complaint. We knew we were walking on holy ground.

Senior missionaries, John and Evelyn Thomas of England, finished their distinguished career as missionaries in Colombia while serving in San Andres. John and Evelyn opened the evangelical ministry in Colombia and had many stories of running for their lives as angry priests and parishioners chased them from town to town because they preached the gospel. Today, both John and Evelyn enjoy the fruits of their labors with the Lord in heaven.

Deyanira came highly recommended to Marilyn as a hairstylist and as she worked, Marilyn had an opportunity to witness to her. It wasn't long before Deyanira made a profession of faith. It was our practice to help new Christians grow in their faith by studying James Crane's book, *My Growth In Christ* which was translated into Spanish. Each week we visited Deyanira at her salon for the eight chapter study. Marilyn always took homemade cookies that Deyanira and her two daughters enjoyed. The youngest daughter, Marilyn, stayed for the cookies and the Bible lesson but the oldest daughter, Patricia, took the cookies and ran up stairs. It took six months to complete the eightchapters but we felt the time was well spent.

A month later after the study, Deyanira returned with her daughters to Bogota and we lost contact with them for five years. After transferring to Cartagena, our last field of Colombian service, I received a call from Deyanira. "Brother

Jim, I have joined a Baptist church in Bogota and want you to baptize me." She had plans to visit Cartagena and could be baptized in the church where we were members. Our pastor, Jorge Campo, consented to the baptism of Deyanira but the more I thought about it, the more I felt her pastor should baptize her and not me. She agreed and told us later she was baptized in her church in Bogota and was happy.

Several years later, Deyanira called again. "I have great news for you and Marilyn," she began. "My daughter, Patricia married a preacher and both feel the call to become missionaries to Spain. They are looking for financial support and wondered if you might help them."

We agreed to help using funds from the non–profit organization I formed after retirement from Colombia. Six and one–half years we helped Patricia and her husband Cesar start and develop a strong evangelical church in the city of Alicante, Spain.

The island of Providence and adjoining island, Santa Catalina, will always have a special place in our hearts. During the years in San Andres we were able to minister to the churches of Providence and its people in several ways. One blessing was seminary extension courses taught by Dr. Bob Adams and Dr. Randall Sledge. Their inspiring and challenging lessons helped the church members grow in Christ and minister better to their people. Several work teams accompanied us to build and repair existing churches. One memorable and effective work team consisted of missionaries Richard and Kaye Rolfe, Delbert and Lois

Taylor, and Ross and Laveta Thompson. Besides the work accomplished, we celebrated in worship and fellowship with island Christians and each other. I won't forget the day I sat on the plane behind my missionary colleagues as we left the island. Turning back toward San Andres, the plane made a steep bank allowing us to see clearly the beautiful blue, green waters that surrounded the churches, palm trees and little red roofs. We set in silence, marveling at God's beautiful creation and blessings.

I had a fishing buddy in Providence named Bush, the husband of an influential Baptist worker on the islands. Bush had fish traps and needed a helper to harvest the catch and that's where I came in. While we trolled out to the traps, I let out my line hoping to catch a barracuda which I often did. Barracuda was fun to catch but you had to be very observant of their sharp teeth and propensity to use them. After getting the barracuda into the boat, Bush immediately killed him with a bat and then cut into the spine to see if he had lead poisoning. If the spine was red he was safe to eat but if black, he had eaten lead from a sunken ship and had to be thrown back into the sea.

Another adventure on Providence was conch diving and our guide was Ovidio Howard, pastor of Central Baptist Church. A piece of glass fastened to a 12' by 12' frame was placed on the water allowing you to see twelve to fifteen feet below. After spotting a conch, you would dive and come up with a catch if you were agile enough. Only once did all the kids go with Marilyn and me to Providence Island. Then all became conch divers, some becoming so good they could come up with three or four conches in one dive. The conch mussel made a delicious stew or salad and the shell was a collector's item.

The Caribbean Sea around Providence was every shade of blue and green surrounded by beautiful coral. Divers around the world visited Providence and swam in the warm waters observing and photographing the vast variety of tropical fish. On my first trip to Providence I met a professor of Marine Biology from the University of Florida who gave daily lectures of the marine life of the island to visiting students from the States. He said these waters were near the top of all islands for having more different species of tropical fish.

Another interesting aspect of the island of Providence and Santa Catalina is their history related to Pirate Henry Morgan of Jamaica. Morgan was a privateer in the eyes of England but a pirate to Spain. Morgan and his men plundered many Spanish ships leaving Cartagena laden with gold, silver and jewels on route to the old country. One of Morgan's excursions was conquering Panama City, Panama making he and his men rich for life. Morgan had an unusual attraction with Providence and Santa Catalina, stopping there often before or after a raid. Today his cannons guard the sea where the enemy might try to enter and a huge rock rising out of the water by Santa Catalina is appropriately named Morgan's head.

One of Morgan's raids took him by Providence but upon arriving saw the Spanish flag flying over the island. Morgan sent a messenger to the Spanish captain telling him to surrender or get blown out of the water. The Spanish captain, a very wise man, sent the following message back to Morgan: "Captain Morgan, I, General Romero Sanchez, commander of the Spanish troops, know we are outnumbered one-hundred to one and we will lose the island if you choose to come ashore. However, you will also lose many of your men in the fight. May I offer an alternative? Could we fight the battle with only gun powder using no bullets or cannon balls? You will win but I can report to my superiors, though outnumbered we fought valiantly." Morgan agreed to the terms, removed all the bullets and cannon balls from their weapons, attacked the island using only gun powder and won the battle with no loss of life. The Spaniards boarded their ships, returned home happy they were alive. A popular belief among the islanders is Morgan's treasures are buried somewhere on the island but never discovered. This is the setting of the first of my three *Hootie* novels.

My first trip to Providence Island was preaching a revival at Rocky Point Baptist Church. I learned neither Providence nor Santa Catalina had electricity except for a few hours a night in down town Santa Isabel. There were only two motorized vehicles on the island: two pickup trucks which were equipped with benches in the back where passengers rode. Rocky Point was about halfway around the island from Santa Isabel and I was ready when the pick–up arrived. I climbed in and took my place.

Down the hill we quickly left the lights of Santa Isabel. After the first turn we were in total darkness except for the dim headlights of the pick–up. We passed one dark house after another until, all of a sudden, an enormous orange ball came popping up out of the sea. As the moon rose it was silhouetted behind palm trees gently blowing in the breeze. I was awestruck and wondered if I had died and was experiencing my first glimpse of heaven. The church's six oil lamps lighted the services, heightening our reverence and humility. I was revived, if no one else was.

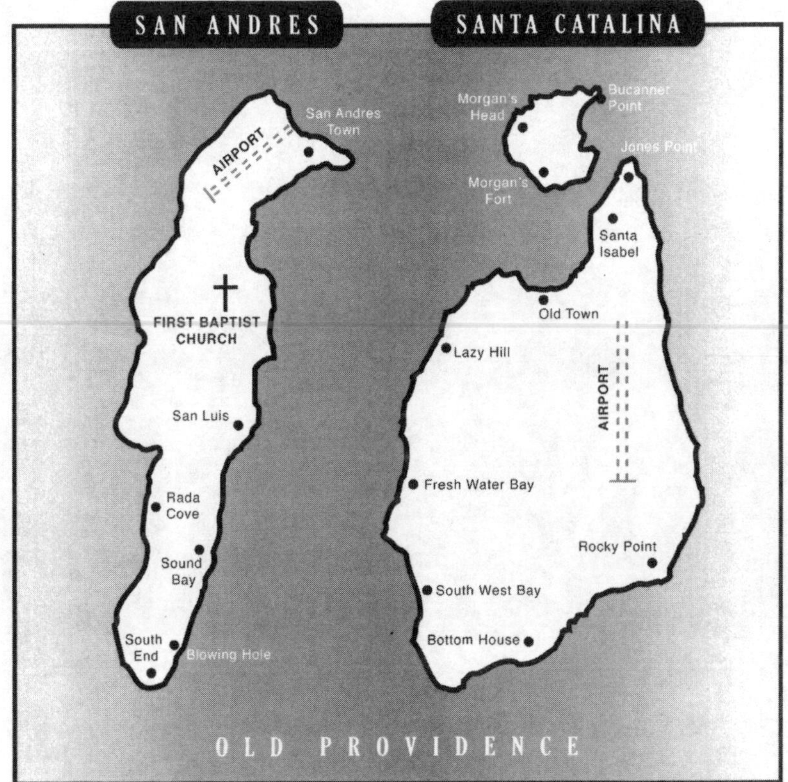

Chapter 26

Goodbye Dad

During our last months in San Andres we received news Dad was in need of more help than his wife and brother were capable of giving. Two years after mom died, dad married a fine Christian named Aribell (Ara) and they had been married fifteen years at the time. Prostate cancer and dementia were causing problems for dad and those caring for him. Ara and my uncle, Sebron, needed help.

After five years in San Andres, Marilyn and I returned to Montgomery where dad and Ara lived. The greatest need at first was taking care of the yard and shopping but by the end of our year's furlough, dad's health began to deteriorate. I requested, and received, a year's leave of absence from the Foreign Mission Board. The Board (now International Mission Board) always helped us in time of need and especially during periods of crisis. We are very blessed to work with such people of Christian love.

To take a leave of absence meant there would be no salary but God opened the door of employment. Riverside Heights Baptist Church in Tallassee, an hour away from dad and Ara, called me as pastor. The members of Riverside Heights blessed us through their love and support during my brief pastorate. Deacons Steve Schmitt and Gerald Elrod kept me busy on my day off looking for golf balls I hit in the woods. They did let me win one game. Clinton Guy was and still is my fishing buddy. It wasn't all games during that year because we were able to teach Master Life (a four month program of Christian growth) and take six members to an intensive study in Birmingham for training in Evangelism Explosion.

During that year dad became weaker physically and mentally and within a few months Ara was unable to care for him. The best for Ara, dad and all of us was for him to be placed in a nursing home and in 1993 he was placed in a modern nursing facility in a town halfway between Ara and us. We visited dad often and saw his dementia get worse. July, 1993 was the date we were to return to the mission field or resign. Marilyn and I needed five more years for full retirement and both Ara and my uncle agreed dad was well taken care of and we should return to Colombia. My last visit with dad was very sad because I knew I probably wouldn't see him alive again. In tears, I kissed him on the cheek and said goodbye.

We had seen the birth and growth of the new Spanish church in San Andres and began praying about our next assignment before we left. Cartagena Baptist hadn't started a new church in twenty years and after praying we felt the Lord leading us to that growing city. Again we consulted with our Area director, Bryan Brasington, and were cleared to move to Cartagena. We were in Cartagena only a month when our pastor, Jorge Campo, came with the news dad had died. Marilyn and I took the first flight back to Montgomery for the funeral.

Dad was greatly loved by many: family, Christian brothers and sisters and State Highway employees where he worked for forty years. It was a very moving and inspirational funeral. Dad was buried in the Daviston Baptist cemetery beside mother and near his parents and many relatives. He had returned home for his final resting place. Marilyn and I have cemetery lots next to mother and dad.

We returned to Cartagena after legal matters of the estate were taken care of. Our daughter, Jeannie, wrote the following poem about her grandfather.

THE PASSING

I saw a quivering
hesitant, wistful
sight
Tonight.

I saw a glimmering
whispering, fleeting
light
Tonight.

I saw your soul
As it wafted out of sight.
You were heading
toward the light.

Grandpa, Goodnight.

Chapter 27

Cartagena de Indias

SPANISH COMMANDER PEDRO de Heredia founded the city of Cartagena in 1533 and named it after the town most of his sailors were from. It was named Cartagena de Indias to differentiate it from Cartagena, Spain. One of the defining features of Cartagena is the three plus miles of walls surrounding the city. San Felipe Castle, a fort that took a hundred years to complete, protected the city and was never captured by enemy invaders after it was built. This engineering marvel with long tunnels and passageways and unique communication system make it a main attraction to visitors.

In the early days, Cartagena was a major trading post, especially for precious metals. Gold and silver from the mines in New Granada and Peru, along with treasures stolen by the Conquistadores, were loaded on ships that returned to the old country. The first slaves were also brought to Colombia through the Cartagena port by Pedro de Heredia.

The key Colombian Baptist leader for forty years was Señor Victor Martinez Corcho, founder and pastor of Alcibia Baptist Church in Cartagena. Señor Martinez was not only a strong leader in the Baptist Convention but also founder of many churches throughout the country. While we served in Cartagena, Señor Martinez celebrated his fiftieth year as pastor of Alcibia and had slowed down considerably.

I became very close to my pastor, Jorge Campo of Central Baptist, who was president of our Baptist Association. Along with Emeterio Gonzalez, we traveled together, starting new churches and promoting evangelism. Jorge helped me start the first Evangelism Explosion class in his church and we saw it expand to other churches throughout our association.

Each year we were required to submit a personal report of our work. The following is our report to the Baptist Convention after our second year in Cartagena. The report was submitted both in English and Spanish.

PERSONAL REPORT – JUNE 1995
James (Jim) and Marilyn Oliver
Cartagena, Colombia

This year was better for us in the area of physical health. We thank the Lord Marilyn's eye is in the process of healing and that she has been able to see better with the help of a contact lens. Wind and bright sunlight sometimes cause pain and redness in the eye but the ophthalmologist has given a good report of the damaged vision. We pray we will continue to stay healthy for the Lord's work in Colombia.

We continue to work with churches in formation, mainly in Cartagena, and hope the mission Dios Fuerte (Strong God), will constitute before year's end. Sunday's attendance is over a hundred and there is a great need for a larger facility. We have also worked in missions of Alcibia, Estrella, Salem and Peniel.

We continue to train evangelists with Evangelism Explosion. At the present time we have certified workers in three of the six Cartagena churches and three workers have been certified in a clinic in Barranquilla. Jim and three teachers are now prepared to take the training to other churches in the Association. Two EE clinics are scheduled for this year – Tierraalta and Cartagena. We are planning clinics for '96 in Monteria and Sincelejo which will cover all the major cities in the Association.

We both participated in two medical evangelistic caravans sponsored by the Clinic Bautista (Baptist Clinic) in Barranquilla. Marilyn assisted Dr. Edwards in surgery (Puerto Libertador) and gave medicine in the other town (Los Cargueros). Jim made evangelistic visits during the day and preached or sang during the evening services. There were evangelistic decisions in both caravans. The caravan planned for Miraflores had to be cancelled due to public disorder. It has been scheduled for later this year.

Glen Cantu and Dena Veazey led a music workshop in Monteria and Marilyn assisted as registrar. The workshop was well attended with much enthusiasm among the participants. The Cartagena Music Workshop had to be postponed until October due to conflicts in schedules.

Jorge Campo, the president of the Association, and Jim made several visits to churches during the year to counsel pulpit committees, install new pastors, explain Convention support plans, help with building projects and plan the total work of the Association at the Executive committee meetings. It has been a joy to work with Jorge this year.

Another unique joy was to preach in a revival and dedication of a new church building in Leon del Medio. This was a mission of Monteria First Baptist Church who built their own building and paid for it themselves. They have a bi-vocational pastor who is helping his members reach new people in their area for the Lord. They also have other preaching points nearby that we hope will soon become churches in formation.

Half of this four–year term is now history. We pray the last two years will be fruitful, not only in Cartagena, but also in the remainder of our Association where the majority of our churches are located. By the end of our tour of duty in Cartagena we saw four new churches constituted in the Association and we praise the Lord. Marilyn and I were in prayer meetings in the home of Luis and Aide Diaz that later became a strong church in their neighborhood with Luis as pastor.

A year before leaving Cartagena and retiring, I wrote the following missionary song that is sung to the tune, "Morning Has Broken:"

FREE FROM ALL DARKNESS

Morning has broken like the first morning,
Light from above that never shall dim;
Sing to the new light that He has given,
Praise for the freedom found in the Son.

Wake every nation to this sweet sun-light,
Let every soul be found in His love;
To Him be praises, Glory forever,
In hearts of peace and joy He shall reign.

Called from above to morning unbroken,
Rise to the Son in glory above,
Eternal light with life everlasting.
Free from all darkness forever more.

Two weeks before we left Colombia we were wined and dined by our missionary brothers and sisters in Barranquilla. They presented us with personal encouraging messages in a beautiful Colombian book along with a painting of Cartagena that hangs in our living room today. Dr. Edwards painted a hummingbird picture for us we cherish dearly. Pastors and leaders in Cartagena gave us a special meal along with Colombian presents. One gift was an old couple sitting on a Colombian porch. He has a white beard and eyeglasses and she's knitting. Finally, we celebrated a special dinner with our pastor Jorge and wife Febe in the romantic, inner city of Cartagena.

June 4, 1997, we were taken to the Cartagena airport by our close friend, Ensign Ken Gustavsen of the United States Navy. We checked in for the last time as Colombian missionaries. We would return to Colombia on different occasions but we knew this was the end of our career. Many church members were present at the airport, including our pastor Jorge and newly appointed missionaries Brian and Rhonda Massey. We joined hands and sang, "Bless Be The Tie That Binds." Tears flowed freely from our eyes and beloved brothers and sisters in Christ. Some of those we may never see again on this earth, but we know we'll meet around the throne of God.

Our bags and footlocker were checked thoroughly and x–rayed. We presented our tickets and were given boarding passes and escorted to the waiting room. Fifteen minutes before we were to board, a policeman came to me and said I was to report to the luggage department. There the officer in charge pointed to our footlocker and said, "Open it!"

After it was opened, one of the policemen began tearing the paper from the inside of the locker thinking he might find drugs. Speaking to the officer in charge, I said, "Sir, I want you and your men to know I'm in complete agreement with what you are doing. We have lived in Colombia for almost thirty years as preacher of the gospel and know illicit drugs is the cancer of the country. I'll help take this footlocker apart piece by piece if that's what you want."

I reached down and starting tearing the paper from the other side of the footlocker and immediately the officer said, "Wait a minute." He lifted a couple of items, looked inside and said, "That will do. Lock it up."

We returned to the waiting room and soon the call came for us to board. As we walked to the plane we waved to those standing by the gate and again we couldn't hold back the tears. A most blessed twenty–nine and a–half years of our life was coming to an end. Marilyn and I said, "Thank you Lord for calling us as your missionaries." There are many interesting careers in the world, but to us, the greatest is missionary work. It's been a party, we're glad we didn't miss it. We know too, the best is yet to come.